Business Process Improvement

Sai Gudlavalleti

Business Process Improvement

Copyright © 2022 Sai Gudlavalleti

All rights reserved. No part of this book may be reproduced in any form or by any means—whether electronic, digital, mechanical, or otherwise—without permission in writing from the publisher, except by a reviewer, who may quote brief passages in a review.

Although this publication is designed to provide accurate information in regard to the subject matter covered, the publisher and the author assume no responsibility for errors, inaccuracies, omissions, or any other inconsistencies herein. This publication is meant as a source of valuable information for the reader; however, it is not meant as a replacement for direct expert assistance.

Library of Congress Control Number:N/A

Cover design by Lance Buckley

Printed in the United States of America

CONTENTS

Introduction 4

Chapter 1. Mindset 11

Chapter 2. Basics 21

Chapter 3. Creativity 50

Chapter 4. Current State 54

Chapter 5. Phases 62

Chapter 6. Future State 68

Chapter 7. "Big Data" 77

Chapter 8. Real-World Example 84

Chapter 9. Layers 95

Chapter 10. Improve 101

Chapter 11. What Next? 107

Chapter 12. Six Sigma and CMMI 114

Conclusion 121

Notes 126

Acknowledgments 129

About the Author 130

INTRODUCTION

Every once in a while you need to challenge yourself and learn new things.
—Amit Ray

Business Process Improvement, from my experience, it is the act of helping a business do better financially. Every business aspires to grow their business and run it successfully, and implementing improvements aims to save costs while increasing annual revenue. The goal of each business is different, but the basic need for improvement remains the constant denominator.

Have you ever recalled a favorite recipe and thought you knew how to recreate it without following the actual steps, including specific ingredients, food measurements, and cooking time? Then you find yourself disappointed when it kind of resembles what your intended but isn't as good as it could have been? Why is that? Well, it's because you didn't follow the recipe, the plan, that would almost guarantee a better outcome.

Business processes can be compared to recipes in that they serve to create an output that will significantly contribute to successful business outcomes. If the process (recipe) is created, evaluated for its potential success, and then implemented by all who will be attached to the process (such as a person, department, or team—and even a client), the goals are easier to reach and clearer to all involved.

The standard definition of Business Process Improvement (BPI) labels it as a management practice utilized for its efficiency and effectiveness by various means: discovering, mapping, documenting, analyzing, and redesigning. Other key components include process improvements, such as improved communication, improved handoffs, and improved system integrations. When these methods are used, then businesses can achieve their mission: company growth, efficient workflows, satisfied customers, happier employees, and better company morale.

In this book, I will be speaking to two categories of people, then I will break down the questions based on the personalities who might be asking them. Skeptics and Learners can relate to these questions. Perhaps you see yourself in one or both categories below. I encourage you be open to the valuable information in these pages, no matter which perspective you take.

The Skeptics

- Why learn about Business Process Improvement?
- Why learn about Business Process Improvement from this book?
- What separates this book from dozens of others written about this topic?
- I know what business processes are, but why should I care?

The Learners

- Will understanding Business Processes Improvement more deeply help me find a job?
- Will understanding business processes more deeply enable me to progress in my career?

- I'm a beginner. Why are business processes something I even need to know about?

I will attempt to answer all of these questions.

First, I want to introduce those who are new to the table to the term Six Sigma Black Belt. No, this isn't a martial arts term in the physical sense. Rather, it signifies the mastery of analytical skills valuable to the business world. Six Sigma was developed by Bill Smith in 1986, and the certification program enhances and sharpens skills for those in the field of statistics, financial analysis, and project management. Generally, it's geared toward people who work with quantitative measurements over qualitative markers. Since you are reading this book, you likely already have a leaning toward this side of business. Many of you might be working toward your Six Sigma Black Belt (there are six levels). I encourage you to learn more about this program as it will enhance your work opportunities in numerous ways.

I was awarded a Six Sigma Black Belt in 2014 after completing a course and a project at the end. For those not familiar with the course and project, this means the completion of learning and understanding the core concepts as well as the successful demonstration of applying the concepts in a hypothetical, or real-world, scenario. I describe the details of my project at the end of this book in chapter 12.

Having focused extensively on Business Process Improvement projects for more than four years, I have a solid understanding of the basics and have gained the necessary expertise to pass on this knowledge through this book.

The world functions on "processes"—business or otherwise. The moment you recognize this, you will understand the importance of a process and the need to improve it. People I know have gone to extreme measures to improve their daily life. But going to extremes is not always necessary in order to boost productivity, live a better life, and eliminate time-wasters and other elements that cause stress.

I have the advantage of perspective to share with you because I've been on both sides of the learning curve during my career. I started out being totally removed from the topic of Business Process Improvement, to eventually working and thinking on these strategies constantly during the projects I've been involved in. Through my experience, I understand what it's like to not know the basics and then be thrown into the fast-paced, high-expectation job that doesn't necessarily prepare you for success. Most of the time, you have to find opportunities to learn, mentors who want to pass on knowledge, and information from books in order to become adequately equipped to succeed at your job. Luckily for me, I had great mentors who were patient and taught me almost everything I know about Business Process Improvement.

My first interaction with Business Process Improvement began as a humiliating lesson, highlighting what I didn't yet excel at. I was assigned to work with a consultant named Bob, who worked for one of the top four consulting firms. From what I remember, he gave me a drawing or something he had sketched out and asked me to put it in a Visio (software that designs business-related diagrams). I remember my first process flow. The result was disappointing: short, ugly, and basic. Since I was neither familiar with the basics nor did I have proper guidance, it turned out to be a very rudimentary design. I still remember it to this day, and the memory of it always make me cringe a little. But I am proud of how far I have come, so if you are new to Business Process Improvement, take it from me. You can do it too!

Bob gave me feedback on how to make process flows look professional, but he wasn't around for long; he was gone after a week. But from his prompting I got my first taste of high-quality, impactful process flows. After that project ended, I got the opportunity to work for two managers, Shrey and Reno, and things were never the same. Most of my knowledge, as well as the shapes and arrangement of them, came from Reno, who was a senior consultant at the time. Shrey was the project manager who asked critical questions and taught me how to see the big picture in what I did. I am incredibly grateful to both of them as they provided the basics for me and helped me excel. They were the coaches I didn't realize I needed at the time. And I could not have asked for anyone better than them to guide me and view processes in such an interesting perspective.

Who Is This Book For?

- You are training or mentoring someone on your team or within the organization.
- You want to refresh your basics skills if you are already experienced, possibly learning a thing or two while reading the book.
- You have no idea about business process flow and have been thrown into a challenging project.
- You are looking to pursue a career in Business Process Improvement.
- You have participated in Business Process Improvement as a side project and are curious to learn more.
- You have an interview for a senior position and want to understand the big picture.

How Is This Book Different from Other Books on Business Process Improvement?

I honestly don't know the answer to this one, and there is a good reason for that. I did consider researching how other business process books were written and structured, but I felt I would be doing a disservice to myself, and to you as the reader, if my writing style was influenced by anything other than my experiences and my perspective. I wanted this book to be as authentic and as "me" as possible without my examples and insights being altered by someone else's formula. Everyone's experiences are unique, just as everyone's way of explaining things is unique. So I thought it would be best to simply lay out the words according to how I feel they should be expressed so you know this is *me* speaking to you. I want this book to feel like we are having a one-on-one conversation, and I am hoping it accomplishes that.

Why Did I Write This Book?

First off, I feel very strongly about improvements in general. I really enjoy everything that goes into the discovery process, where we take the time to learn something new, interact with different systems and personalities, and most importantly, create the future state. After successfully completing a few diverse projects, I wanted to share my findings and experiences to benefit others who were in the beginner stages, as I enjoy mentoring and guiding other young professionals who are new in their business career. And what better way to accomplish this than documenting my findings and putting them into a structured book? Plus, I had always secretly wanted to write a book because I've been avid reader since I was a child, always devouring whatever I could lay my hands on. Fiction was my primary choice as a child, but as I grew older, I read non-fiction exclusively, particularly enjoying business books. I finally sat down to write, and if I'm honest . . . it was daunting. But it was also exciting after I put pen to paper as I finally began my journey to become an author.

My goal is to provide a no-nonsense, concise way to approach business process flows, and I hope this book will provide you with what you are looking for.

Sincerely,

Sai Gudlavalleti

CHAPTER 1:
MINDSET

*You have power over your mind—not outside events.
Realize this, and you will find strength.*
—Marcus Aurelius

Step One: Prepare Your Mindset

It is very important to have an open mind. At best, go ahead with a blank slate. Having preconceived notions is going to limit you and your thought process. As you will see in the following chapters, you will understand the power of asking why. If you have older children, go back to the time when they were three years old. You were likely asked a why question every five seconds, and they would not let go till they were satisfied. You have to think like a three-year-old: curious, wanting to understand, only letting go when there is a satisfactory explanation. Go in with a blank slate and you will thank yourself later.

Industry-specific knowledge is both a boon and a curse. All industries pride themselves on hiring specialists. This is great if they already know what problems to solve and if they want to create a strategy for the future. Specialists are undoubtedly great for that. However, they are often so forward-thinking that they miss simple solutions and overlook some of the simpler problems that sit in the present moment.

Being an industry novice/rookie is, however, very rewarding. There is an opportunity to question the fundamentals and "shake the core." You will be amazed at how often you will hear, "We have always done it this way." As often as this cliché has been used in multiple blogs, LinkedIn posts, and in business meetings, this outdated mindset continues.

Entering an industry with no prior knowledge will ignite in you a fundamental curiosity. Human beings have always been a curious species. Imagine if we were not curious, then we would not have gone to the moon, discovered the Internet, identified numerous varieties of fruits and vegetables, unearthed precious metals, and created synthetic materials. (Regardless of how you feel about plastics, look around and see how indispensable they are in everyday life. If you are still not convinced, I recommend reading *Stuff Matters* by Mark Miodownik.) So don't be hesitant if you get an opportunity to work in a new industry. Your contribution will be beneficial for both parties as interesting insights will be revealed. Having some knowledge will help but is not necessary.

Why is a mindset important when approaching a particular task? Because we are only as limited as much as we think we are. There are countless stories that have shown how people have overcome their limitations and achieved success. A lot of obstacles had been thrown at them; they endured difficult situations, were met with contempt, and everyone doubted their success— but they kept at it and achieved what they intended.

Achieving success has never been easy. Being born with a silver spoon presents opportunities in the initial stage, but only hard work ultimately makes a person truly successful. It is easy to look at successful people and think they have had it easy, but that is far from the truth. Having a dream is not enough; effort must be put in as well.

Step Two: Set a Lofty Goal

Be realistic, but don't sell yourself short either. If you don't think highly of yourself, no one else will. What do you want to accomplish? What are your short-term and long-term goals? Remember, no one has to know or see if you have it written down. The idea is to have it handy when you are feeling lost or feel like you are wandering from your path. Or maybe your goal is there to inspire you. Being motivated is a very important step in reaching your goals. I can say from experience that it is very easy to stray from your path and abandon your goal. A personal example I can share is me striving to write this book, which took about a year on and off to finally complete. You may not reach and acquire everything you set out to do, but by implementing the methods in this book, you will get as close as possible. Even if you fail, you don't have to learn and accomplish above all others. Always hold the comparison to yourself. Be the best version of you!

Step Three: Look for Opportunities to Learn

There are different and various ways to consume content. Data generated over a hundred years pales in comparison to the data generated over the last few years. With the rise in social media and traditional outlets, there is no dearth of quality content over the Internet. There are a ton of experts readily available to teach and coach us on any specific subject, ranging from basic math to astrophysics. You are just one click away. According to US Chamber of Commerce Foundation article published in 2013, 90 percent of the world's data was produced in the previous two years.[1]

Now you have choices on how to consume data. In the past, you would have to know people, go to libraries, and read. Now you can stay at home and research, learn, watch, and listen to whatever you want. The key is that learning never stops. If someone says they know everything there is to learn about a specific field, that is not someone you should be taking advice from.

Step Four: Network

We live in a world that is connected like never before. There are multiple platforms you can connect with and engage in professional discussions. By being a silent observer, you can learn a lot. But when you have questions, feel free to ask. You'll be surprised at how many people will step forward and help. Teaching and helping are two qualities every human being has, whether or not they like to admit. You'll never know what you might learn or discover, or what opportunities you find, unless you stay engaged and curious.

Step Five: Practice

This is probably the most important step. Regardless of how you feel, all you have to do is show up and keep at it. You would be surprised with how much you learn as you master the art, as you will see in later chapters. Business Process Improvement is both an art and a science. It takes time, but remember that Rome was not built in a day. Observe and read about all the successful people today. They might be smart, but there is no substitute for hard work—even though they may say or think otherwise. Every successful person would tell you how many hours they have spent practicing their craft, which made them the success they are today.

Wouldn't it be great if we did nothing and everything fell in our lap? Unfortunately, we have to put in the effort to get the output we want. The more you practice the more you will get better at something. Refer to the 10,000-Hour Rule that Malcolm Gladwell wrote about in his book *Outliers*.[2] That's right, 10,000 hours. How soon did you give up when you tried something? Even if it's hard, remaining steadfast will likely result in an amazing learning experience and successful outcome.

Step Six: Set Up Your Process (tools and prep)

There are a variety of tools you can use to document and keep track of your processes.

Depending on the complexity of your processes, you can use PowerPoint or Visio. Note: If you have some heavy-duty process flows you'll be cranking out, I've had the best experience with Visio. Can that tool be improved? Absolutely. After using it extensively, though, I'm very comfortable with it and prefer it unless someone recommends a better tool.

If your organization has a template, I would recommend using it so every document stays consistent and everything looks organized. Keep the template handy when you begin a new process to reuse the shapes, then try to avoid straying from your default template. If you feel there is a better way to represent something, or if you have proven best practices from a different organization, feel free to make that particular suggestion. With applications being updated every few years, there is always an opportunity to use new features to avoid making your process flows look dated. The goal is to have all process flows follow a pattern, so having a template designed at the organizational level helps keep all documentation consistent within the department or organization.

If you are a freelancer or looking to learn about business processes, create a template you can reuse. This will make you look polished, organized, and professional. I cannot stress the importance of having a template that is well-defined. Creating a template should be your first step when starting from scratch. Tip: Draw on paper before you begin drawing on Visio as it is easier to draw your thoughts on paper than in a tool. There is something magical when you go old-school and use a pen or pencil to write on paper. If you haven't tried it, give it a shot. Thoughts come freely, and you will not get as easily distracted. If anything, freehand writing will energize you. We live in a world full of distractions and "buzzworthy" notifications on the twenty devices we have. Put them all aside, and you will be surprised at how much better you can do.

Always start with the big picture. Once of the scope of work has been identified, use a project management tool to document and keep track of all your documents. This is extremely important to ensure everything is and stays on track. Also, this allows you to provide a status update at any point in time when asked for one.

Depending on the preferences, a status report should be created. This could be done in Word or PowerPoint. As long as I can easily see the status and it is displayed with details explaining why a particular process is being delayed (if that is the case), a PowerPoint deck is not necessary. I will not go into detail on project management tools, but they are very useful. You can research which platform best suits your needs by doing a quick online search of the top ten most recommended project management platforms. It is also important to have an accompanying Excel document. If you want your process flows to look like art (as you can see in future chapters), this Excel file will serve as your science. It will capture everything that is on your Visio process flow as well as everything that is *not* on it or *does not belong* on it. I will provide an example of everything that has to be on the file, along with sample columns. And don't worry, you don't have to be a pro in Excel for this. Basic skills, such as in typing in cells, is more than sufficient.

Attestations and Signatures

An attestation is evidence of proof that something has occurred. When you are requesting an attestation, you are requesting confirmation that everything has been completed to the satisfaction of the client, and they are signing off on the document/deliverable that you have created. It is important to always have written confirmation to ensure an activity took place. In our scenario, a process flow was reviewed and everything looks good with no changes required. By attesting the document, the client is saying, "Yes, I have reviewed this document and agree with the content."

Another general example of attestation is when you are filling out an application for a job and provide your professional and personal information. At the end, you are required to attest that all the information you have provided is true to your knowledge. This means if you have provided any false information, you are taking responsibility and will be denied from either applying again or will have to face other consequences.

Attestations can be completed on paper or digitally. Depending on how the organization or sponsor prefers, all documents should be signed by the Subject Matter Experts (SME) that have been interviewed. This will ensure a successful completion of the project with blessing received from the interviewees.

Documentation Collection

As part of any project, collection of all documentation is as essential as any task. This ensures all related parties are aligned, and the project could be easily referenced any time in the future. You can go a bit further and timestamp your documentation. This will help preserve your work and provide an easy way to look for it, should you need to refer back to it or if you need a little inspiration in the future. It may even tell you how you could do something better or how you have progressed. You might even learn a couple of things on what not to do. It also helps to show professionalism if you collect them and present as one project instead of simply a collection of documents. Always double-check that your files and folders are appropriately labeled and stored in their related folder. I was given a wise piece of advice relating to this topic: "When you show a process flow to someone you randomly encounter, they should be able to read, understand, and tell you what is happening."

Scheduling

You have to schedule meetings with the subject matter expert to understand what is currently going on in their departments. A subject matter expert (or SME, pronounced "smee") is someone who has extensive knowledge in a particular area. These are the people who have been working on or researching a particular topic for a long time and are expected to have the answer for everything in that field. For example: Neil DeGrasse Tyson is an SME on astrophysics. Daniel Kahneman is a SME on behavioral economics. They are brought in for discussions so they can offer their valuable feedback on ideas and concepts. These people are masters of their particular subject, and their insight is very valuable, especially when you are considering changing certain processes.

A SME will be identified and assigned to your project, so you don't have to worry about finding this person yourself. Sometimes during the course of a meeting, you may identify someone who has more working knowledge with their experiences, so never consciously or unconsciously rule out anyone's opinion or advice.

Depending on what the organization uses, you should be able to use that software to schedule meetings. It can be Microsoft Outlook IBM notes or Google Suite. Understand what is available in advance. This will help in planning ahead and cut down your preparation time should you need to learn something new or reduce the time you need to create a process flow to meet your deadline when you have a meeting with your client. A good rule of thumb to follow: once to gather information; the second time to review.

If you have to meet the same SMEs more than three times for the same process flow, then you are not paying attention *two times in a row*. This does not give a good impression. Remember, everyone's time is valuable, and if you're going to improve processes, the thing they will tell you is that your process can be shortened to save time. Don't fall into that predicament. How do you do that? Through your senses.

Senses

Yes, this is the tool you need regardless of what else you have. You need to pay close attention to what people are telling you. Recall the saying: "You have two ears and one mouth; therefore, you should listen more and speak less." This is especially true in the beginning, when you don't have enough knowledge about the industry or particular department you will be working with.

Speak only to ask questions during the interview. You will be amazed at how much information you will receive. Your goal is to capture as much as you can. Remember, there will be a lot of terminology and jargon coming your way. Don't hesitate to ask what you don't know.

Summary

1. Mindset is key. If you have the right frame of mind, you can achieve whatever you want.

2. Set goals and ask yourself how you can accomplish them. There is plenty of information and hundreds of smart people on the Internet who have already achieved what you are planning to achieve.

3. Network. Everyone is within reach. It is only you who are restricting yourself. If you believe in the theory of six degrees of separation, you are already connected to the person you are wishing to reach out to. In today's age of social media, it would be really hard not to find the person you are looking to network with.

4. Provide consistency in documentation. If you don't know what all you need, look for documents that have been used within the past in the organization. If none exist, then you get to create your own and leave your signature!

5. Use your senses and don't be afraid to ask questions. Since we evolved from hunters, we are naturally designed to pick up verbal cues, body language, and other signs simply by staying alert and paying attention to our surroundings.

CHAPTER 2:
BASICS

By failing to prepare, you are preparing to fail.
—Benjamin Franklin

In this chapter, we are going to focus specifically on the basics. A good setup goes a long way in eliminating having to do your work twice. Avoid simple mistakes that could get overlooked in the immediate moment but will definitely stand out (in a bad way) when you are not prepared later on, such as in a presentation. Preparation is key in this instance, and this chapter talks about everything you need to create a process flow. The goal here is to ensure you are familiar with the shapes, layout, and everything else you need to create a process flow that is not just clearly understood but is one that you will be proud of. I will also cover some basics on project management, which is required to help estimate the time you need to deliver your project on time.

Always begin with a thirty-thousand-foot view. It helps to see the entire organization or department from a unique perspective the first time. Don't get nervous after seeing the big picture. Use it to determine how to strategically break down the entire chunk into manageable processes. How do you eat an elephant? One bite at a time. Use this methodology for your process flows as well.

Project Management

Begin using building blocks to create an outline for all the process flows that you believe should be defined at the highest level. Once they have been defined, you can start breaking them down into multiple processes that collectively make up the high-level process. Once you have this overview, it will be used as your guiding outline to help connect your sub-processes.

Take some time to create the outline. This can be drawn on paper and later transferred to Visio. Once you have the outline, create high-level tasks for them in Microsoft Project or Excel. Assign dates, identify your SMEs, and schedule two sessions—one for capturing information and one for review. It's probably best to go a bit granular and list the sub-process to get a better handle on how much time this process will require. Doing so ensures you're blocking adequate time in advance with the SME. Do not space the two sessions too far apart. A review session should always be done while the process is still fresh in their minds, so space them closely. Each process flow should have at least one of these components:

- File name
- Process name
- Description
- Swim lanes
- Actions
- Decisions
- Arrows
- On-page connectors
- Off-page connectors

You know what they say, "A picture is worth a thousand words." So let's start by looking at some basic shapes and the tools you will use to create your process flow diagram.

File Name

Once you have the processes identified as part of the project, be sure they are labeled appropriately. Don't randomly name them as 1, 2, 3, etc. An efficient and clear way to group processes is by naming the category, then use the actual process name. Having to file and reflect which process they belong to makes it easily searchable. The last thing you want is to keep digging through folders to find the document you are working on. Create appropriate folders so they can be easily accessible by anyone. Even those who are not familiar with the structure should be able to find the documents just by looking at the process name. Also, ensure that the file name of the accompanying Excel sheet matches with the process flow. They both go hand-in-hand, so it's only logical to name them the same. You could add "_Description" at the end of the Excel file to keep them visually separate.

Page Setup

We might be moving toward a completely digitized world; however, there might be certain instances where a physical print is being required. It can either be for reviewing or for getting signatures. Sometimes it is easier to review documentation when it is on paper. There are two reasons why the right page setup is required. First, for presentation reasons. When presenting a process flow, you should have the right size for display. All of the shapes should be visible clearly within a page. Second, should someone want to print and view this document offline, they should be able to do so effortlessly. Having them struggle to print a document does not look very professional.

What has worked for me very well is the following setup:

- **Page Size:** Legal works best because it ensures you have enough real estate to capture all of your actions and decisions. Letter can work if the process is not very complicated. However, you would not be getting the project if it were simple, right? Legal size should also be easily available, though not as plentiful as Letter, but let's not let that deter us, eh? Anything larger than Legal size becomes a hassle to handle, so Legal hits the sweet spot, being both practical and big enough for documentation.

- **Landscape**: Ensure the orientation is set to Landscape. Again, you could use Portrait, but it will limit the space you have on your page, especially if you will be using Legal (it will look funny when you view or print it).

- **Print Preview**: I usually add this icon to my toolbar because I monitor how the process looks when I print it, and it lets me know if I am staying within the layout. Doing so is not a necessity, but saves me going through hitting Print and seeing it in that window.

Process Name

This should be the name of the process being worked on—reviewed and presented. Ensure the document clearly indicates the verb "tense." It should be labeled as "Current State" or something along those lines.

Description

As it suggests, this section should give a brief description of what this process does or is trying to accomplish. It can also include descriptions of acronyms that will be used in the process flow. More on that later in "actions." Try to keep this high-level. You will have all the details in the Excel sheet, which will match what's on there as well. Again, any employee (even a stranger you ask at random!) should understand what this process does by just reading the description and without needing an explanation.

Depending on the version of Visio you use, this is how you can find the shapes if you are creating a new template or are creating a process flow from scratch. When you open Visio for the first time, select the option for "Basic Diagram." I use U.S. units but you can choose metric depending on where you live, and then select "Create." Note: For the purposes of this book, you will not see anything related to units.

You might have some default shapes selected, such as arrow shapes that are vital to your document. If they are not selected, go ahead and select them. You will have a plethora of options to choose from. Always remember to pick one and stick to it. Too many options are not always a good thing. It can get confusing and waste your time; however, if you are the type who wants to experiment and see what you like, more power to you!

Go to the left menu and under "More Shapes," select "Business Process" and then "Six Sigma Flowchart Shapes." I chose this because of the standard, and it's helpful when we stay consistent with everything else. Or if you prefer, you can select BPMN standard shape. You can find this under "Flowchart," then "BPMN Basic Shapes." More on Six Sigma and BPMN later.

In my examples, I chose both to give you a taste of how different it looks if you go with a standard option and if you customize it. Play around to see what suits your style best.

Another important shape you want to select is a swim lane (coming up next). Select "Flowchart" and then "Cross-Functional Flowchart Shapes." This should give you your horizontal and vertical swim lanes.

If my directions to find the shapes are hard, you know what the best option is . . . Search!

Fortunately, there is a search option in Visio. Depending on your version, there is a "Search Bar" where you can input the shape you are looking for, and voila! All options will be presented and will be saved in your history. This helps in not having to go searching for a shape every time.

Another quick way to have all of your shapes handy is to add shapes that you most commonly use to your "Favorites." It's another way of saying you can "create your own stencil." This is one of the funky Visio things I am not a fan of, but if it is something you can appreciate, go for it. I understand the intent; however, I prefer to have my favorite shapes saved and easily accessible as opposed to having to save it as a stencil. This eliminates an additional step of finding and opening the stencil to use.

Swim Lanes

Swim lanes may be arranged either horizontally or vertically. I arrange them in a vertical format because that has worked best for me. It paints a nice picture, flows left through right comfortably, gives me the real estate I need to capture all elements, and overall is visually appealing. I would recommend using the vertical format (you will see this style in my examples).

Think of runners as you watch them run from left to right. Without making it too complicated, let's just say they run one lap. This is not a race. They start from the left and finish at the right. They're doing their own thing and running at their own pace. Now, this is perfectly fine since they don't have to coordinate with a quartet, communicate with anyone, or time themselves based on other runners. Remember, this horizontal swim lane does not signify a race.

Let me define some terms for you if this information is presenting itself for the first time:

- **Swim lane:** A swim lane is a graphical container for partitioning a set of activities from other activities. BPMN has two different types of swim lanes. See "Pool" and "Lane."[1]

- **Pool:** A pool represents a participant in a collaboration. Graphically, a pool is a container for partitioning a process from other pools or participants. A pool is not required to contain a process, meaning it can be a "black box."

- **Lane:** This refers to a partition that is used to organize and categorize activities within a pool. A lane extends the entire length of the pool either vertically or horizontally. Lanes are often used for such things as internal roles (such as a manager or associate), systems (an enterprise application), or an internal department (shipping, finance, etc.).

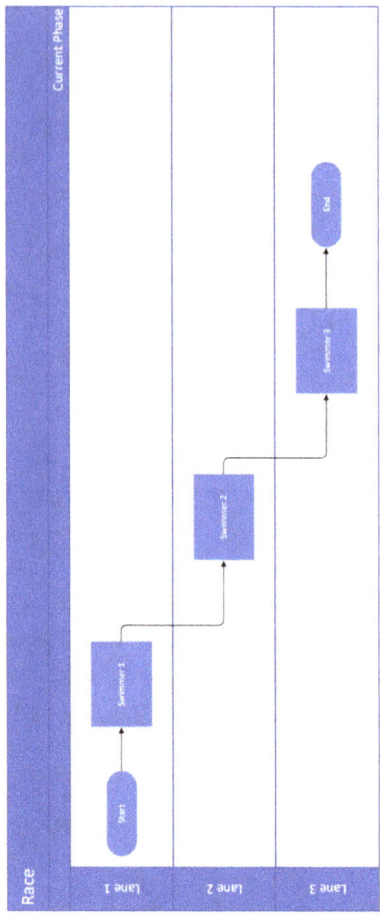

Now let's say it's a relay where runners have to pass a baton. All runners are dependent on each other. The only way they can get ahead is if they receive a baton from the previous runner. The second runner cannot move until they receive a baton from the first. The third runner cannot move forward until they receive a baton from the second runner, and so on.

This is what a vertical swim lane would look like:

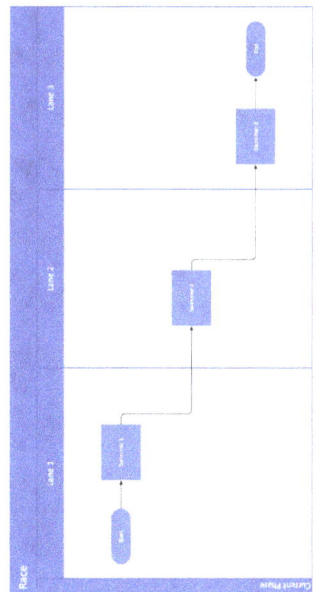

They might look very similar at first glance. This is because I'm using a very simplistic example to show how the process flows from beginning to end. Once you start getting into complex flows, it will look different, and how they read will depend on what you are used to.

As you can see, everyone has a different starting position. But they cannot take an action until they receive the baton.

This is how it usually works in the real world. Every department has different responsibilities. If you want to look at the high-level picture of an entire organization, you will see how departments interact with each other to accomplish a goal.

Let's take a look at the assembly lineup at a car factory. I will offer a very simplistic view of the process so you can better understand this concept.

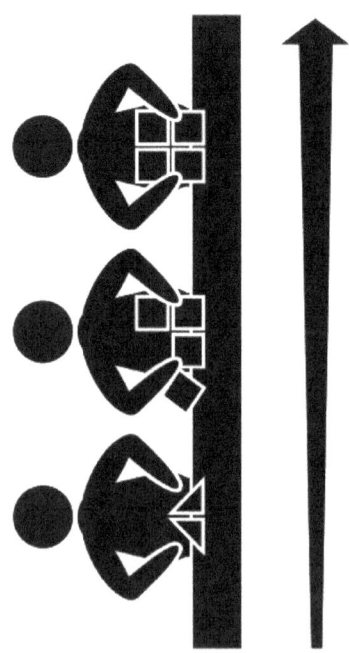

Again, keep in mind that this is just one department, and we are assuming only one person is doing this work of assembling.

Actions

An action is defined as the "accomplishment of a thing, usually over a period of time, in stages, or with the possibility of repetition."[2] From a process flow perspective, an action is performed by the user or system, depending on what your process flow is. Every process flow is a combination of basic actions and decisions that our user encounters in order to move to the next step.

When outlining actions, I like to start with a verb. This clearly indicates what action is being taken. Once you start doing this for every action, you'll soon realize the power of consistency and having a clean, professional-looking action box in your process flow. Actions are usually depicted in a square box. All shapes indicate what they are doing. A good rule of thumb is to have the same size for all action boxes. Having different box sizes makes your process flow look unorganized, as if not a lot of thought was put into it.

In order to make it visually appealing and ensure it flows smoothly, set aside time to create well-structured action boxes, and use them moving forward. I will cover stencils and creativity in later chapters.

To summarize, what you need for action:

1. Square box
2. Set size
3. Start with a verb

A good rule of thumb is not to have two of the same actions in a process. If that happens, it means it is a *redundant action*. Also, try not to have the same two verbs in an action box. What do I mean? Here is an example:

Actor: Human

Action: Check accompanying (file name) Excel sheet for grammatical errors

Actor: Software (Ex: Grammarly)

Action: Check accompanying (file name) Excel sheet for grammatical errors

See there? That's what they call a penalty in sports! Jokes aside, you can see a red flag there (oops, another sports reference). And this is the message I am trying to get across. The joke's funny the first time, but not the second time. Similarly, if you catch two people doing a similar action, capture that in your current state and ensure you highlight that as an improvement opportunity in your future state process flow.

Let's start off with a simple example. In this case, driving a car to work. You will see there is an opportunity to improve mundane things, such as the simple, everyday action of driving to work. So you follow the basic steps of taking your keys, driving, and reaching your place of work. How does that look when you put it into a process flow?

Basics

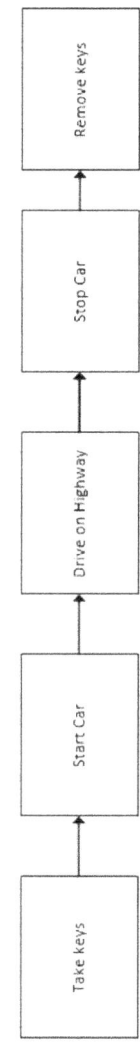

Decisions

There will be times when a user or a system will have to make a decision depending on the choices they are presented with. A quick search will tell you that on average, people make about 35,000 decisions a day. Let that number sink in: 35,000. This could include what to wear for the day, what to say or not to say in a meeting, how to address urgent situations, what to cook for dinner, and what ingredients to use. It's not that surprising once you add them all up.

Fortunately, we won't have as many decisions to think about when designing a process flow. A decision should lead to a yes or no. That's what a decision is for, isn't it? The goal is corroboration. The definition of corroborate is "a choice that you make about something after thinking about several possibilities."3 And this choice is to take one action, not multiple actions.

Try to think of the question a user or system faces in these basic terms. If a question requires a decision that turns into multiple options, there's a way to depict that in a process flow. Depending on the scenario, I could offer multiple options on how this could look. For now, let's assume there will only be two outcomes, two choices, or two paths to take—depending on the question.

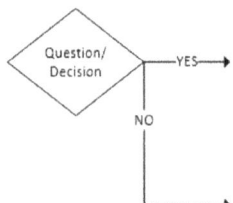

Just like actions, you should never have to make the same decision twice. If you see that happening in the same process more than once, it should immediately make you think about improving it. This is different from a peer review, but you can have two or maybe three different people look at the same thing to review for errors and consistency.

As you have seen, we make a lot of decisions every day. We shouldn't have to make duplicate decisions now, should we?

Building on the car example, because I like to keep things simple, here is an example of how to implement a decision in a process flow: In talking about the car, you saw how a decision was incorporated. You should not have to check for gas twice if you can check it right after you start your car. If someone is doing it more than once, that is a good example of process improvement. Why? Because the driver is now free to think of other things during the drive and not worry about running out of gas and trying to find a gas station. Instead, they can listen to peaceful music or a podcast or an audiobook (ahem) to start the day. This can cause anxiety and stress and eventually lead to some bad driving habits. Which is, of course, not safe for anyone on the road.

Business Process Improvement

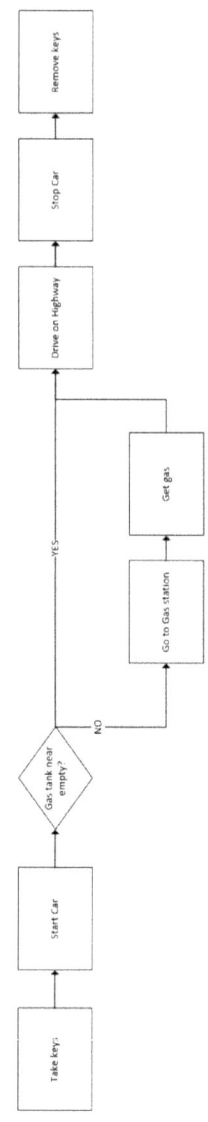

Actions and decisions are the basic building blocks of a process flow. Start building them left to right and think of the next steps as you keep moving along.

All processes technically have a starting point and a finish line. Usually there is never a true start or a true end. Again, let's refer to the car example above: Is there really a start and end? Before taking the keys from where you got them, you had to have put them there. After removing the keys, you probably went to work or were running an errand.

In order to differentiate and separate processes, let me introduce another shape called the sub-process. A collection of sub-process will turn this into an overview. This will be the high level I mentioned earlier. Using the car example, see below to classify and separate process flows:

1. All processes should have a start and end.

2. Ideally, start and end only appear in the overview.

3. Processes are separated by sub-processes.

4. An overview depicts all available processes under a sub-process.

Business Process Improvement

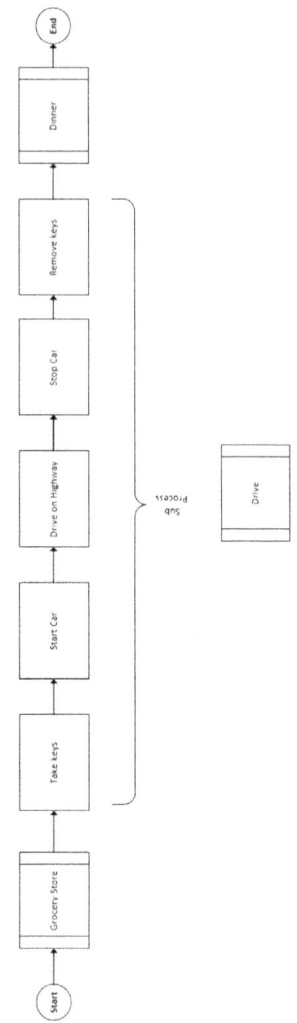

38

zzzzzzzzzzzzzzzzzzzzzzzzzNumbering

Every shape on the process flow should have a number associated with it. This will help in two ways:

- You can follow along when you point out a specific shape and have to go over additional detail.
- You can tie the shape back to details in the accompanying Excel sheet in case someone needs to refer to them.

Should you number these items as soon as you create a shape in the flow? Not so fast! Take a look at the Critical Path section below.

Arrows

These are pretty self-explanatory. They guide our user from one step to another. Since we are covering the basics, let's look at two different types of arrows.

- **Path**

This is the arrow I have used in the example shown earlier. You, dear reader, no doubt understood what was being shown, as this is a very simple action to follow. No, there won't be just three or four actions or decisions on a process flow. If you noticed how I labeled errors when a decision is made, you will see that they can either be labeled exactly on top of the arrow, or you can create a text box on top of the arrow to indicate the path. It is a straight line with an arrow at the end to indicate the direction.

- **System or File**

In order to indicate if a file or system is being used, you can use a dotted arrow. For example, let's say you're sending an email with an attachment using Gmail. This is how the arrow would look:

Notice how I use a dotted arrow to indicate a file being sent with the email. The details of the file will then be listed in the accompanying Excel sheet. Same thing applies to the system icon as well. You can use the different icons available within Visio or PowerPoint to create a visual representation of the systems or files being used in the process flows.

You can provide details around a file, such as its contents, the intent, the font used, character limit, and everything in the Excel sheet. Similarly, you can provide details around the system used, such as its operating system, type of laptop used, and its processing power in the Excel sheet.

To summarize:

1. Use a straight arrow for showing a path.

2. Use a dotted arrow for a system or file.

3. Use icons to indicate systems are files.

Straight or curved?

In my experience with outcomes, curved arrows look much better. The curved version smoothly defines the process flow. I used straight arrows in the real-world example (see chapter 8) since that is a fairly simple process. I would encourage you to use curved arrows by changing the shape and see how that looks.

Page Connectors

A page connector is a shape that is used to link two shapes either within a page or within a document that has multiples pages. It is used to visually show if two shapes in a sequence cannot follow each other in a straight line. When you start adding shapes, you will face a situation where the arrows get jumbled up because of actions that are bouncing back and forth between the same actors. This is where a page connector helps in clearing out the space and giving it a clean look.

An on-page connector is a shape that is used to link shapes within a same page, just as the name indicates. For you to be able to use this, your connected shapes should live within the same page. If, in the course of adding new shapes, you notice that the connection will be lost, meaning the second shape in the sequence will move to a different page. You cannot use the on-page connector shape anymore. You will have to use an off-page connector.

If you cannot wait to see what the one stood for, I don't blame you. I may have done this in the past because, because as you might have assumed by now, I'm generally very curious. It won't disrupt the flow, so whether or not you read it in order does not matter.

Business Process Improvement

As I mentioned earlier about the stencil and printing guidelines, it is essential for a process flow to look professional and be print-ready.

As part of those principles, I use page connectors to link one action after another if I'm running out of space within a page. Take a look at the two process flows below, then decide for yourself which one looks better and cleaner

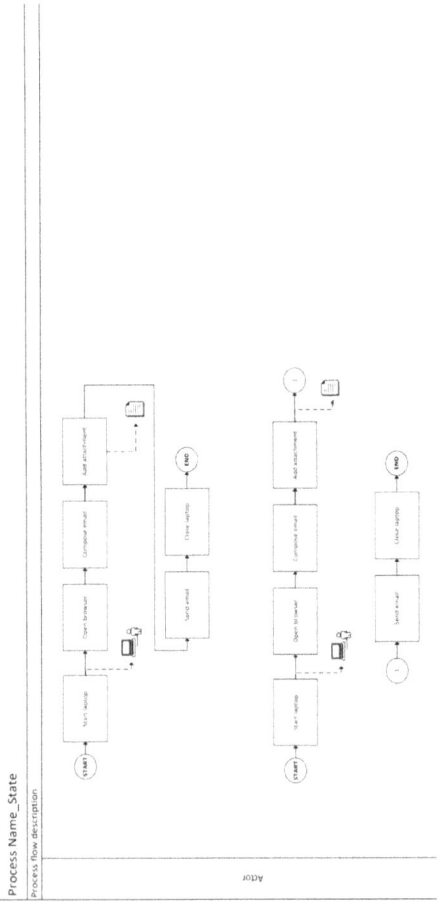

Not only is more space saved on the flow, it also looks very clean. Once the on-page connector is explained, it will become very easy to follow.

Off-Page Connector

An off-page connector is a shape that is used to link multiple pages (or tabs) within a single document. It is used to show the connectivity between actions or decisions that span multiple pages. There could be scenarios where a process on Page 1 has run out of space and takes multiple paths that require their own pages. This is where an off-page connector would help when you have to connect Page 1 with Page 2 and also Page 1 with Page 3. Confusing? It's easier to explain with pictures and examples that you will see later in chapter 8.

Keeping with the principal off of clean flow, this shape can help you jump into a different page by double-clicking the shape. Typically, they are used for process flows that take more than one page to document. There are no hard-and-fast rules about keeping a process to a single page. As long as it looks presentable and everything is captured, there should be no issue with having a process flow that takes more than one page to document.

There are two kinds of off-page connectors: outgoing and incoming.

- **Outgoing**

Sometimes it is possible that a process flow takes more than one page. In order to link multiple pages, you can use an off-page connector. When presenting, you can quickly jump to the next page to show connectivity.

This is what outgoing connectors should look like:

Business Process Improvement

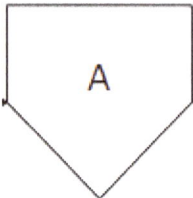

- **Incoming**

Similar to outgoing connectors, this shape indicates that the current page has a link to a previous page. Note: A page can have both incoming and outgoing shapes. I use numbers for on-page connectors and alphabets for off-page connectors. This helps them stand out and allows the viewer to easily differentiate between the two connectors.

This is what incoming connectors should look like:

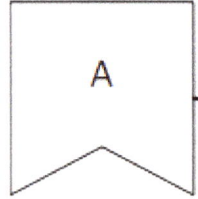

As you will notice in the example I provide in chapter 8, there will be numerous and varied shapes on the page. It would behoove you to distinguish between an off-page and an on-page connector. Sure, once your eyes are trained, you will know which is which. Remember, we talked about anyone being able to read it and follow the flow? The shapes should be fairly simple to follow. However, if you do number them, following along will become much simpler. Imagine a scenario where there are multiple on-page connectors on a page. Even you would do a double- or triple-take if you did not number them. Except for start and end shapes, it is best if all shapes are numbered so that when you glance at a page, you can quickly see where one flow ends and another begins.

Let me offer a quick example of a football field (American or soccer). Players have numbers in a large font size on their backs and their last names in smaller font size. This is because it makes it easy for a referee to quickly identify which player incurred a penalty or foul. They won't have to figure out someone from the back or have the time to read the name. All they have to do to identify the culprit is see a number.

Using that analogy, if you noticed the shapes in my example above, you can see that I numbered my on-page and off-page connectors. Now, if you were really paying attention, I used numbers for on-page connectors and letters for off-page connectors. Why is that? There are three reasons: First, it's how I learned and continue to use it that way. Second, shapes on a page are all numbered. If there is a letter, it is a giveaway that the following steps or actions do not belong and will be on a different page—since a letter sticks out and is visually representing something that is identified uniquely on a page. Third, the goal really is to distinguish between the on-page and off-page connectors. You could theoretically number both shapes; however, it is best to differentiate between them to avoid confusion. You can use letters for on-page connectors and numbers for off-page connectors as well—as long as you know how the shapes are connected and if someone looking at them knows what shape comes next from reading the flow.

Next is where you'll really want to use BPMN standards because the shapes that I have used will vary from what is listed in V2.0 (as of the date I am writing this book). BPMN also calls them "Throw" and "Catch" (in case you wonder why

I used a football reference above). This is what their shapes look like:

As you can see, if you place more than one of these on a page, it will require you to look at both a couple of times to see which ones they are connected to. If you use the shapes I provided above, adding a letter to distinguish between the on-page and off-page connector, it will eliminate confusion. Just by glancing you will be able to ensure everything is connected to the right shape.

Critical Path

While creating a process flow, you'll notice that adding a decision can branch out into separate paths—and not just from a numbering standpoint. You also have to think about which path offers the least resistance. Also known as the Critical (Happy) Path. Let's use our car example to determine the Happy Path.

Basics

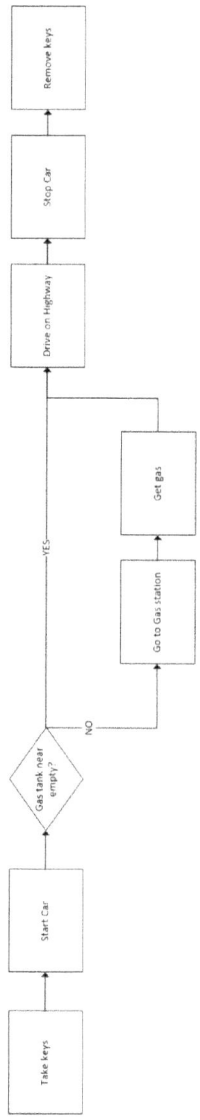

As you can see, the easiest path is if everything is going well. This is named is the Happy Path. Why do we need to call out a Happy Path within a process? As I mentioned, one advantage is for numbering. Once you have the numbers down, it will help in adding the required detail in the accompanying Excel sheet.

Let me offer another way to think about critical paths: once you have identified the easiest path to get from start to end, anticipate other pathways that a decision could potentially lead to.

BPMN Standards

Business Process Model Notation (BPMN) is a standard that is globally utilized to document a business process. It is an open standard based on a flowcharting technique and can be customized to suit preferences. For more information, I highly recommend going to their website for more information on specifications and certification options.[4] I have adhered to this standard and modeled my process flows based on it. It doesn't mean you have to do the same, but it will help you look professional and be consistent throughout.

Summary

1. Be consistent. Choose a standard and stick to it.

2. Ensure you understand all of the important shapes you require to build out your process flow.

3. Project management is key. You have to have a target in mind and must be able to estimate how long your document will take to produce. This includes interviews and any additional meetings and reviews.

4. We make a lot of decisions every day. Try to minimize them wherever you can.

5. Know your shapes and how to use them. This will help you stay focused on the goal.

CHAPTER 3:
CREATIVITY

Creativity is more than just being different.
Making the simple, awesomely simple, that's creativity.

—Charles Mingus

I felt it was important to dedicate a chapter to creativity because I feel strongly about it and how important it is—not just related to business processes but about everything in general. The definition of creativity means "relating to or involving the imagination or original ideas, especially in the production of an artistic work."[1] I don't agree with this definition though. Specifically, the use of the word "imagination." Somehow, imagination and creativity are always used in conjunction with one another. To be creative does not mean you have to be imaginative or come up with original ideas. Sometimes you can come up with great ideas that are not necessarily "out of the box"—no pun intended given the chapter we are in.

There is a lot of creativity involved when you must expand on the verbs used in an action. This includes the number of words you can use so that everything fits in a predefined box, action, or decision. The real creativity comes to the forefront when you start running out of space in a page, but you need to fit in one last action box. Sometimes the best examples are the ones where we actually work hands-on.

When I was first recommended to be creative when working on my first process flow, I chuckled silently. Yes, I admit I was initially a skeptic too. After a few process flows, however, I realized what it truly meant. Sometimes you must stretch your creative muscle when you are in a sandbox, and there are limitations.

Don't be discouraged if you are an entrepreneur who has not yet come up with an original idea or done something that is "out of this world." We are all creative in some way or another. Given the right opportunity, we let those creative juices flow where it matters most to us.

Neurons are nerve cells that send and receive signals from your brain and are constantly firing, carrying information throughout your body. In a sense, we are always "working."

Still don't believe me? Take a look at the examples I provided in chapter 8 and see if you continue to disagree. To create art, you have to be creative, right? So to create a process flow that looks like a piece of art . . . Well, you get the idea.

Creativity is inherent. You were born with it. Everyone is. It's not as special as it's made out to be. You just choose where you want to use it.

Manipulation. What does that word mean to you? It is almost always used in a negative connotation, especially when it comes to human emotions. Let me present a different take on it.

The dictionary definition of manipulation is:

1. "the action of manipulating something in a skillful manner"

2. "the action of manipulating someone in a clever or unscrupulous way"2

What should have caught your attention (since I mentioned a different take above) should be two words in the two definitions: *skillful* and clever. It implies the manipulation of something or someone to achieve a desired result. If you are doing it for the benefit of someone or for the greater good, what is wrong with that? Doesn't sound too bad now, does it?

Let's look at a couple of different examples:

Example 1: A ten-year-old

They want something. They know how to get it. They know if they ask one parent what the answer would be, and they can guess a similar outcome from the other parent. If it's not going to be a straightforward, favorable response, they know how to get it from that parent. They know what to say, but not by asking directly, which eventually leads them to getting the object of their desire. Some may call it manipulation. Some may say they got creative and achieved what they wanted. Which side are you on? Did they "read the room" and plan their approach with the odds favoring them?

Example 2: Jewelers

Twenty-four-carat gold (pure gold) is a soft, malleable metal and is not conducive to create jewelry, watches, or the like. So it has to be mixed (manipulated) with a different metal, such as iron, to create a stronger alloy, which is now eighteen-carat gold. This alloy is now stronger, less corrosive, and has better resistance to day-to-day activities that involve exposure to air, salt water, and other strong and hard materials. Not everyone can do this; only skillful artists or artisans can. Do we call them creative or manipulative?

Clearly, creativity is a skill that can be developed over time. In fact, there is nothing that can't be learned and developed over time with practice. Skills fall into that category as well. No matter what you want to learn, practice is important. And practice makes perfect. What you need is just the mindset that you can do it. I would highly recommend reading *Mindset: The New Psychology of Success* by professor Carol Dweck. She goes into detail about a growth mindset versus a fixed mindset. It's a fantastic read that gives insight into how we are wired and how can we change things if we feel they are not optimal.

Creativity is just another skill that needs your attention and interest. And you are already on a path where you think differently and are willing to create tangible change. Don't let anyone make you believe otherwise. We are all creative regardless of the field we are in. Creativity is definitely not restricted just to arts, such as music and painting. Use creativity wisely to benefit yourself or someone else. Use it in the true sense of the word, and let it guide you in all your endeavors.

Summary

1. Being creative is not restricted to a profession.

2. The best creativity emerges when you are restricted.

3. Creativity is a skill that can be developed over time and with practice.

4. We are all creative; we just don't all know it.

CHAPTER 4:
CURRENT STATE

The world will not evolve past its current state (of crisis) by using the same thinking that created the situation
—Albert Einstein

What is the Current State? The definition of current state means "occurring in or existing at the present time."[1] In the context of this book, Current State is a straightforward, no nonsense view of how a business process works today. No assumptions should be made, and no judgement should be passed. It is an attempt to capture the ongoing state of affairs as it currently happens as accurately as possible.

In this chapter, we are going to focus on the first set of deliverables that will be required as part of the Current State. All previous steps should have been completed prior to beginning this documentation. The project must have completed the signature state, timeframe for completion, and the total number of deliverables must have been agreed upon. What is the immediate step after this before you start creating your flow?

Scheduling Interviews

Ideally, the length of the first interview should be limited to sixty minutes. This time allotment is the sweet spot. Anything more and you risk getting sidetracked; anything less and you will not have adequate time to ask and answer questions. Keep in mind that interviews involve not just your time but your stakeholders' time as well. Everyone complains about how meetings intrude upon productive work hours, especially if they are not productive. In order to maximize their efficiency, it's important the meetings (or interviews, in this case) are well-defined and to the point. In other words, they should be productive. So how can we accomplish that?

First and foremost, planning is key. After the high-level scope has been finalized, you will need to identify all the processes and sub-process that will be a part of the project. Determine which processes require interviews, and identify the stakeholders associated with that particular process. For maximum productivity, limit the number of stakeholders who come to a particular meeting. Doing so will help you stay on time and will limit the focus to the topic of discussion. Ideally, you want to interview the person who does the work as opposed to someone who oversees it. There are nuances and workarounds people tend to use when they are the ones doing the everyday tasks and projects. These are the people you should be talking to because they are the ones who will provide accurate information for the process they follow every day.

Determine who you wish to speak with, and then schedule the first meeting. Ensure you have had enough time to prepare prior to meeting with them. Remember, you want information from them, so ensure you know what you need to know instead of figuring out what to ask them once they come to your meeting. It goes without saying that you would need to determine everyone's availability. If schedules clash, you should prioritize meeting with the person who is most essential, and schedule the meeting based on their availability.

When you schedule the meeting, ensure the subject is accurate and the meeting has a clear agenda. There should be no confusion about the topic and the desired outcome. The first meeting will be about identifying the Current State. To help you better understand the substance required in first interview, I have provided a template:

Subject: Project Name_Process Name_Current State_Interview_Round 1

If the subject name becomes too long, try variations and see what works. You could also use "workshop" since it is a collaborative effort and the participant will be talking a lot. As long as the participants understand the purpose of the meeting, framing the subject in this manner should be sufficient.

Agenda (body of meeting invite):

As part of Project_Name, you have been identified as the SME for Process_Name. We will be conducting an interview to understand the current state of this process and will be documenting responses.

Ideally, you will be sending out the review meeting invites along with the interview meeting invites. The schedule may have already been mapped out by your lead, and they will let you know which deliverables are due during which week of the project. In case it has not been mapped out, a good rule of thumb is to meet with them for review within seventy-two hours. This way, the goal and process remain fresh in everyone's minds. And just so you don't forget, the accompanying Excel sheet with the Current State should be sent out as well. Since the interview has not been conducted, you can use a template and get your audience familiarized with it. This is a deliverable that will be required as part of sign-off. For a completed Excel sheet, refer to chapter 8.

This means you will have seventy-two hours to complete and get your process flow reviewed internally. No pressure, right?

For reviewing the process with the SME after the interview, you can use the following template:

Subject: Project Name_Process Name_Current State_Interview_Round 2

Agenda (body of meeting invite):

As part of Project_Name, we will be reviewing Process_Name for interview conducted on MM/DD/YYYY to confirm understanding and/or address any errors in the documented process flow to ensure its accuracy.

A good rule of thumb is to send an agenda within twenty-four hours of the meeting. In this case, you can add the agenda when you send out the invite as the agenda is pretty straightforward.

Preparing for the Interview (Round 1)

We talked about Visio preparation in chapter 2. For the interview, you won't need to have the template ready because it is only going to involve learning about the process and taking notes. What is required, however, is that you do some homework prior to meeting with the SME/SMEs.

Once the invites have been sent out, you need to get the basics ready. Do you have any prior documentation you received from the SME? This could be something that was created by them or by a consultant. It could be a process flow in a Word document—such as a Policy and Procedure document or a Desktop Procedure document used for newly hired employees or for compliance purposes. If you did receive prior documentation, I would highly recommend reading it thoroughly. It serves two purposes: a) it helps you understand their existing process, and b) it will save you time—in two ways. How? First, you will know what questions to *not* to ask since they already provided specific information, which saves time in your meeting. Second, you can start creating your process flow without having to wait for the interview. The catch here is that the information needs to be relevant and not outdated. Confirm with the SME that this information is appropriate to be used for your project.

If there is no documentation or the existing documentation cannot be used, no need to worry. It is actually good if you don't have anything. Making assumptions is not a good thing, since there are questions you will not ask if you assume you know certain things. A simple example would be communication: assuming it is done via email when it could be done through a workflow. Remember, there are no dumb questions. You are looking at it from the outside and are genuinely wanting to know how a certain action is done.

If you or your lead has prior experience with a similar process, you can use it to get a better understanding of how the process works in general. However, a process within the same industry, such as health care, is done in a different way. So never assume anything.

Now what kinds of questions would be the right ones to ask? Like I said, there are no wrong questions, just don't ask obvious ones. What you will notice is that every has their own language; therefore what one term means in one industry will have a completely different meaning in another industry. In these times, it doesn't hurt to ask or confirm what it means. In other words, it's okay to ask what it means in layman's terms, and I'm sure they will not mind telling/explaining it to you.

After the Interview

It is always a good idea to document the key points mentioned in a meeting and distribute meeting minutes or meeting notes to the group that participated in the discussion. It is fairly common that certain action items that may require follow-up after the meeting. These action items could be following up with a certain individual either because they could not attend the meeting or because they have additional information that the current participants cannot provide. Documenting the action items and ensuring you have that information ready will make the next meeting go much smoother.

Action items are essentially items that could not be addressed during the meeting. To keep it simple for the purpose of this book, here is how a basic layout reads: *Item #, Description, Name, and Due date*.

This will ensure everyone understands what is being requested and when it is due. A good rule of thumb is to send the meeting minutes within twenty-four hours of the meeting. For process flow purposes, since you will be reviewing a picture with them, you don't have to worry about sending your interpretation or sketches along with the minutes.

Once you have your notes and all information gathered from the interview, go ahead and start updating your process flow. If you have the template, it will be easier to copy your shapes and keep adding them as required. You're on the clock, so make every action count!

Preparing for the Interview (Round 2)

Ideally, the length of this meeting should be thirty minutes. Remember, the goal of this meeting is to confirm everything that was mentioned in the first round, including all of the follow-up information that was required after the initial meeting concluded. As mentioned earlier, this meeting will ideally be held seventy-two hours after the interview, so hopefully you will have a fairly decent amount of time to complete your process flow, get your reviews completed (see chapter 5), and be ready for a final review of the process flow with your SMEs.

You will have something tangible to meet with your SMEs this time, both process flow and Excel sheet documents. Go over the process flow with them to get the high-level idea right. If you have questions, you would have annotated them and marked them so you wouldn't miss it. This should be fairly simple if you have documented everything as they had described in the interview session. If there are minor edits, let them know you will make those changes in the next version.

This should conclude the documentation for the Current State.

I want to mention an important fact here: you will barely speak during the Current State. At this point, you are only gathering information and will be limited to asking questions and letting the client/sponsor speak. This is how these sessions should be designed because your aim is to understand what is happening without having to do a lot of work. Let the information first come to you. Even if something surprises you or doesn't sound right, write it in your notes but *do not* deviate from what the client/sponsor is telling you.

Summary

1. Current State is documenting the here and now without making any assumptions.

2. Schedule interviews and prepare for them by gathering any available documentation.

3. Rule of thumb is to have a review session 48 to 72 hours after initial interview.
4. Focus on gathering information for the interview. Listen more; speak less.

CHAPTER 5:
PHASES

Phase is a necessary evil. Unless you come out of one, you will not know what lies on the other side.
—Anonymous

The definition of phase is "a particular appearance or state in a regularly recurring cycle of changes."[1] In this chapter, we are going to see the different phases an artifact or document (in this case, a process flow) goes through before it is considered completed—from its inception to finally getting it signed off. It may sound simple, however, to keep things moving along because you will be going through all of the phases, and a couple of them may not be fun. This ensures your document is as error-free as humanly possible and includes all the potential scenarios (limited to the scope of course) of any particular action or decision.

Just a note that there will be a similar yet slightly different number of phases for Current State and Future State. As you will see notice, Future State process flow will not have to go through as many reviews as a Current State. This is because you will be using your Current State document to create your Future State document so the focus of the Future State document will be primarily on the improvements, since the typos and little things have already been ironed out in your Current State document. Also, the process may differ based on where you work. If there are fewer phases, then it will reduce the time spent on the documents;If you do have the luxury (money) and flexibility (time) to incorporate all of them, it will be money and time well spent on creating a near flawless document.

There are typically five phases you will go through for a completed process flow. This will apply to your accompanying Excel sheet as well.

Draft

This is when you create your first version of the process flow after the initial interview. Remember, you could be interviewing multiple departments. You could gather them at once, but sometimes you won't be able to pull them all together. During a scheduled one-hour interview, one department might do the majority of the talking for the first forty-five minutes, leaving only fifteen minutes to cover all the steps the other departments are taking as part of that process.

Use the down time between your interview sessions to start working on the first version. It does not have to be pretty; it simply has to capture everything that was recorded in the interview sessions. This way you will have a leg up in the next interview session to (if possible) confirm your findings from the previous session.

Revised

This could be the second or third version, depending on the number of revisions you require after completing your interview sessions. Ensure you are capturing the revision numbers on the file name of your document to avoid confusion. Thoroughness is key with your revisions. Ensure you have captured all possible scenarios, all potential pathways, and all players associated with the process flow. You don't have to get everything right, but you should not have simple mistakes in this version either. Don't get called out on simple things, such as having the wrong shape or shape size or duplicate numbers. Refer to chapter 2 if you have any questions about the basics. After this revision is complete, you should have very minimal edits. However, don't worry; it does not have to be pristine. The next step will help explain why.

Review

There are two levels of review that your document will have to go through to ensure it is of the highest quality—meaning as error-free as possible.

- **Peer Review**

If you are working as an individual contributor, you will not have the luxury of getting your process reviewed. You can, of course, consult with someone to do a quality check of your process. If you are working within a team, you are in luck! Schedule time or have them review it on their own.

There will be times when things are strictly opinion-based and there is no right or wrong way to do certain things or approach something in a way that is different from yours. What it boils down to is preference. If you are confident of what you have in there and know it will work, don't worry about upsetting someone. Don't listen to someone only because it's not your viewpoint. If you ask for a review, then it would be rude to not listen to their feedback because they spent their time reviewing your documents. No one is trying to win; everyone is only thinking about how to make the end result better. It's okay to have your opinion because you are the one who knows your audience, and you are the one who did the interview. This situation is inevitable and can get a bit frustrating, but the end result will be a higher-quality product.

- **Supervisor Review**

If you are reading this book, it's likely you are new to the job or have a junior role within the team. Once it goes through peer review, there will be a third and final quality check of the document to ensure there are no important pieces of information that have been left out. Usually, a more experienced person will be reviewing at this point. As a result, the review is more high-level, and their feedback will help you understand how to connect other dots (processes) within the project.

Final

This is the final version of your document. All feedback from peer and supervisor reviews has been accounted for. If spell check has not been turned on, now would be a good time to do so to guarantee there are no typos that may have been overlooked during the review. Ensure your font and the font and shape sizes are consistent. The last thing you want is a client finding a typo after all the effort you put into your documents. This is the last step, and you should try not to go over this document again until you are presenting it.

Presented

This is an optional phase. You can use a different version of the final document solely for presentation purposes. This is where you can add arrows or callouts or layers to demonstrate specific points in the process where you will be recommending changes. Depending on the audience, you can tailor your document to make it more visually appealing. Again, this is an optional step, and you can avoid it altogether if you are running short of time.

Version History

Documenting version history is always important. If someone wanted to see what changes were made to a specific document throughout the history of the project, version history would be a good reference point. It's very rare for someone to look at the version history of a document though. It typically gets examined when someone is looking for an excuse to fault something or someone. When not used for fault-finding, this is one section of the documentation that is purely for tracking purposes. Sometimes it is helpful when a client forgets a certain suggestion or input or decision they provided. Referring to the version history that has the date/time, meeting session, and a name that specifically mentioned something takes out the guesswork. Furthermore, these decisions will help the project move forward when a similar situation arises.

I would recommend adding a tab in the Excel sheet to capture version history. Since this is an all-text file, you should have no problem documenting it here—but be as detailed as possible. Try not to add too much text when including annotations on the Visio document because a) there is no right place for it, and b) it would mess with the aesthetics.

Important to note here is that all of this is a manual process. Everything from you interviewing, documenting, and reviewing all of these artifacts. While you are going through these phases, it is very natural and common to see that sometimes everything starts to blur and look the same. So there are things you might miss after looking at a document three or four times, which is why it is important to have someone else look at your documents so they can recognize when something looks off, or to provide a different perspective. Is there a way to improve this manual process? Glad you asked! I can think of one:

Record Your Sessions: If the client is comfortable, you can always record your interview sessions. This will ensure you can go back and capture things you may have missed during the first go-around. Although I will counter this by saying that having to relisten to the conversation may zone you out, and this valuable time may be used elsewhere.

Are there other ways to do this? Absolutely. But there is a reason why this is such a manual process. Every business process is different, and there is no set template you can use when documenting or reviewing a certain artifact. It is possible there is a software that can scan a handwritten process and create a base process flow that you can work off of, but I am not aware of such a thing. If there is one, more power to you if you can make it work!

Summary

1. Phases are important as they clearly demonstrate progress between different versions of your documents

2. There are typically five phases your documents will go through: Draft, Revised, Review, Final and Presented

3. Version History and capturing changes is critical as that helps in understanding changes made to all the documents. Also, you need to know which version to use depending on your audience

4. Recording a session is helpful but not necessary. The goal is to capture as much pertinent information as possible.

CHAPTER 6:
FUTURE STATE

The best way to predict the future is to create it.
—Abraham Lincoln

Future State is defined as "time that is to come"[1] In a business sense, it is hard to find an exact definition, so I went with the one that was the closest to what I intended to portray and one that is very relevant to our discussion.

In this chapter, we are going to look at what we are getting paid for. Jokes aside, this is where the rubber meets the road because this is exactly what you were brought on or hired to do: learning and working on basics; getting your mindset right; learning about people, their roles, their day-to-day activities, and the issues they currently have that will hopefully be "resolved." The Future State document may or may not solve all their problems, but you have to get as close as possible to help put them in a position where they can agree with your recommendations and set them on a profitable path—depending, of course, on what their goals with this project are.

The best part about this document is that you have a solid baseline to build off of. Depending on the number of improvements you identify, this document may not change much. But again, the Future State document will differ for a small business that is just starting out or has been operational for a few years compared to an organization that has been performing fairly well for over a decade.

Congrats! The hard work has been done. You are now ready to move on to the next state. This is the time you will take to reflect on your findings and focus on improvements. Schedule your Future State review meetings well in advance. Allow enough time for your SMEs to be present at these critical meetings. Remember, once these improvements are recommended and presented, it will become the new normal for a lot of the departments.

The recommended improvements must be:

- Well-researched (Always cite your sources, but you don't have to reveal past clients' names and other confidential information.)
- Well-thought-out (You must be able to explain your thought process on why you are recommending a particular change.)
- Well-presented (Sometimes presentation makes all the difference. You will be able to get your point across if you understand how your client/sponsor thinks or approaches a particular situation.)

Start looking at the process flow, and its accompanying Excel sheet, one process flow at a time.

As part of the interview process, you will have identified some of the improvements. This could be the client or part of your observation while capturing the Current State. Certain steps might seem like they can be improved. However, that might not be entirely true. This is why you need to review them with the SMEs before presenting them to higher management.

Note: In this chapter, I will use the word *steps* to refer to both actions and decisions. This will ensure I am covering both and will avoid confusion if I am referring to one or the other.

Some of the usual suspects that can be improved upon include:

- **Manual Steps** (steps that can be automated by using a system)
- Example: taking notes in a notebook and then typing them again in an online system.
- **Duplicate or Redundant Steps** (steps that are performed twice by different actors)
- Example: review of the same document by people in different teams that does not show a significant change in outcome.
- **Unnecessary Steps** (steps that are not required or that seem forced)

Example: locking a car multiple times.

Remember: You don't have to recommend improvements just because you're expected to do so. If your findings indicate no changes are required, it's okay to say so. In fact, you can complement or mention instances where the client/sponsor has already made improvements in the past and/or where they have already made an improvement knowingly or unknowingly.

Sometimes redundancy is good. Are you wondering how? Let me explain.

Your car has four tires, which is all it needs to function properly. But you also have a spare tire in the back "just in case," right? You have your keys in your pocket, but you've been walking around a lot, being more active than usual. You feel for the keys in your pocket a few times just to be sure they are still there. That's redundant behavior. You know you put them in there, but it "doesn't hurt to look." In case they aren't in your pocket, you can retrace your steps and find them.

But when the stakes are high, such as with a team that is preparing to launch a rocket, calculations are done twice by two different people, nuts and bolts are double- and triple-checked. Multiple rounds of quality checks are conducted to verify parts, calculations, communication systems, etc. Is it redundant? Yes. Is it critical and necessary? The answer is a resounding yes.

It all boils down to what is necessary and what is not. In some cases, rechecking is only done to ensure peace of mind. To take emotion out of that equation, let data guide you. Determine the cost and amount of time it takes. Once you have that, weigh the pros and cons to decide if it is worth the additional cost and/or time. If not wanting to fail is the ultimate goal, especially if a life is involved, then it is definitely worth the cost and/or time.

Let's start highlighting where improvements can be made to the Current State. You can reuse the accompanying Excel sheet to highlight and make necessary notes so you have the documentation ready. There are multiple ways to highlight and identify the steps that require improvement. You can:

- Select the text in the action or decision box and highlight it in green (more on the color later).
- Color the border of the action or decision box.
- Make the border of the action or decision box weighted for enhanced visibility.
- Use a combination of the above.

Since I haven't yet discussed the proper placement of color within a process, let me offer some advice. If you want to call something to attention, you could color that item red or some shade of red. Using the same methodology might also bring about negative attention because red often signals that there is something wrong with that action or decision; therefore, using that color might elicit a defensive reaction.

What you are looking for is buy-in from your SMEs. You have to walk a fine line between offending them and getting them to understand why you are recommending an improvement to an action or decision. Once you navigate through the dynamics and are successful in explaining that the improvements are for the better, it will become an easier conversation. Personally, I prefer using green because it is easier on the eyes, does not scream for attention, and does not imply that the action or decision is wrong.

Let's continue using the car example to identify improvements in a Current State process flow. If you observed carefully, you may have already identified one improvement that can be made. Go to Step 2 and highlight it in the Visio diagram. (You'll notice I used a combination of border color and weighted border.) Note: This is a basic function in all of Microsoft programs so I have not included instructions for this. Below is what the Current State process flow would look like:

Once you have all the pieces identified and highlighted, you will only have to walk through the items that make your presentation easier and smoother to follow along. Once you have identified the recommendations in Current State, you can then create your Future State process flow. Based on the car example and the recommendation you identified, this is what the Future State process flow would look like:

Future State

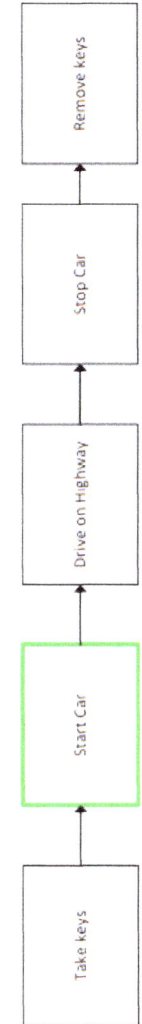

Business Process Improvement

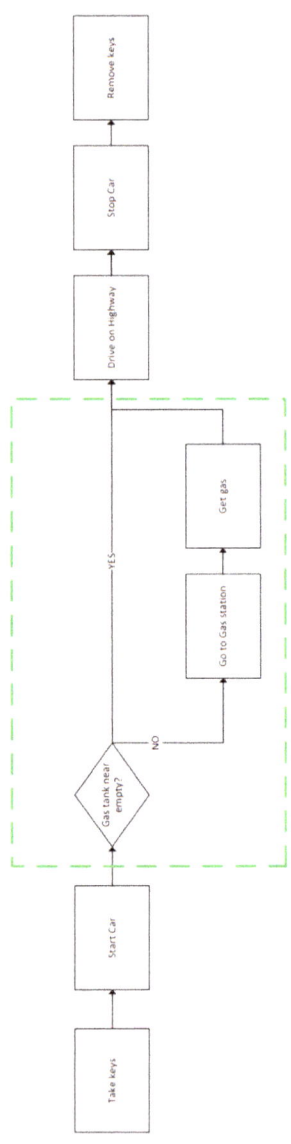

Note: The outline I created is only to highlight for educational purposes. Since this is a fairly simple example, it may look okay. However, you don't want to do this for your real-world projects. This is where layers would enhance the impact of your process. Layers automatically direct the eyes toward what has changed from Current State to Future State.

There you have it. The mythical, hypothetical Future State document that will define what the future should look like. It can be simple or complicated depending on the process. Take additional time, if you can, and double- and triple-check all of your observations and opportunity areas. Sometimes it is easy to assume and overlook simple things only to find out they are the deal-breaker and what is hurting the department or organization. I understand there is pressure to perform here, but such is the case everywhere. Just focus on getting your basics right, verify them with someone in a more senior position, and don't resist going back through the "phases" if required. There is a downstream impact if these recommendations get implemented, such as changing the training system or rearranging job responsibilities; therefore attention to detail is critical here.

Summary

1. Some of the improvements have likely been identified during an interview or documentation for your Current State document.

2. Identify the usual "offenders," such as manual, redundant, or unnecessary steps.

3. If you have industry benchmarks, don't hesitate to include them in your documents.

4. Highlight the shape that has been changed and/or requires improvement.

5. Call out a shape or a set of steps that have been going well and should continue to follow that path.

6. There will be people who are sensitive (physically and mentally) to colors. Try to find colors that are easy on the eyes and don't evoke strong reactions.

7. A Future State document is only as simple or as complex as your Current State document.

8. The effort to create a Future State document would depend on multiple factors. There would be a difference in operations and improvements in a small organization versus a large organization.

CHAPTER 7:
"BIG DATA"

Data beats emotions.
—Sean Rad

Data is a very commonly used term these days. There are multiple positions for business titles, such as data analyst to data scientist to data/tech evangelist. There are organizations that even have chief data officers who have multiple teams dedicated to analyzing data and ensuring quality data is gathered and presented. So why is this important to a business process flow?

Depending on what you are trying to accomplish, data plays a very significant role in Business Process Improvement. Big decisions are made based on data and associated numbers. To enter a new market, an opportunity analysis is conducted. To test a new product, samples are released and feedback is gathered to determine if it is a feasible and financially viable opportunity. To check if a sales department is meeting their numbers, sales data is analyzed. If a team or an organization has to grow, shrink, or be eliminated, they take a hard look at data to make some very important decisions. Annual performance assessment for certain jobs is also measured based on outcomes and the results they are producing.

You could be a one-person army and take on analyzing data for your process flows, but be careful making that assumption. As you have been advised before, never make assumptions, especially around data. For the purposes of this chapter, I have not included a detailed data analysis as it can get overwhelming. I will focus on data collection and preliminary analysis with regards to process flows.

This gets into a complicated discussion because even though data collection is easy, analyzing it is much more difficult because of how it can be interpreted or misinterpreted. Capturing data is pretty straightforward. At every action or decision, ask, "How long does this take?" You should arrive at your answer quickly. For simple actions, you will get simple answers, such as, *Entering data in an Excel sheet for fifteen lines takes about ten minutes*, or *Typing feedback after a customer call takes five minutes*.

Yes, I know these "answers" sound very simple, but be careful of the complexities involved in arriving at this juncture. Entering data for fifteen lines does not factor in worksheets, columns, and whether or not any formulas are involved. There could be multiple scenarios here, and trying to document how many categories of documents there are requires updating. Similarly, a customer call can take five minutes to fifty minutes. This could be due to difficulty in speaking with the customer or because of a technical issue.

Decisions are sometimes dependent on the number of people involved in making them. If it's a supervisor who has to make a decision in five minutes because a customer is on hold, there would not be a lot of discussions involved. Now imagine a purchase an organization is making for software or a consulting engagement that could be anywhere between $500K to $1M. Would that decision be made by one person in five minutes?

As you can see, it can get complicated pretty soon as you keep drilling further and keep peeling the onion layers. Be careful about your time and total commitment to the project, including deadlines. Scope is therefore crucial and must be agreed upon prior to beginning the project. This will ensure you stay on track and avoid delays to your project, such as going down rabbit holes.

Just to be clear, trying to get clarification and going into deeper discussions is not a bad thing. If an opportunity presents itself, add that to the scope of your project and go the "Change Management" route to get it approved. To simplify, *change management* for the context of this book means you have to define the additional work you will be doing, why you are doing it, how long it will take, how many people are required to do it, what it will cost, and if the sponsor is willing to approve the additional expense. If time and money are not an issue, you will have more work to do. See, it's not a bad thing, right?

Now there is no cause for worry if the additional scope for data analysis does not get approved. You can ask for an approximation from the SMEs and document it. Remember, you are going off of what they are telling you. Don't assume or document your assumptions in any of the actions or decisions for the Current State. You don't know their current processes and are only documenting what they are telling you. Make sure to annotate or document in your Excel sheet that it is an estimate provided by (insert SME name) and if there is a reason why they think it is the best estimate. The devil is in the details, so keep the documentation as tight as possible. Leave guesswork out of it wherever possible.

As for the analysis part, you don't have to be a data expert to be able to do this. No fancy tools are required nor do you need to be technically savvy to analyze data. While defining the scope, determine if a data analyst is really required. Nine times out of ten, you should be okay. However, it really depends on the project you will be working on. With that being said, you should view this expanded scope as an opportunity to dive deeper into the process to get an exact understanding of how the process works and the time it takes to make a refined, educated recommendation on how it can be improved.

Great, you received approval to conduct data analysis. This is where you get to fully flush out a process and get the true picture. The best way to document the time required for each step (process or decision) is . . . you guessed it: in the process flow itself, including a brief description using an annotation, and within the Excel sheet, which has the details. As mentioned before, ensure you have defined and estimated beforehand how long capturing data for each process would take. It's okay if your estimation is off by 10–15 percent, but not more than that. It will seriously jeopardize your deliverables and ultimately your deadlines. Here is an example for how to document in Visio using our existing car example:

"Big Data"

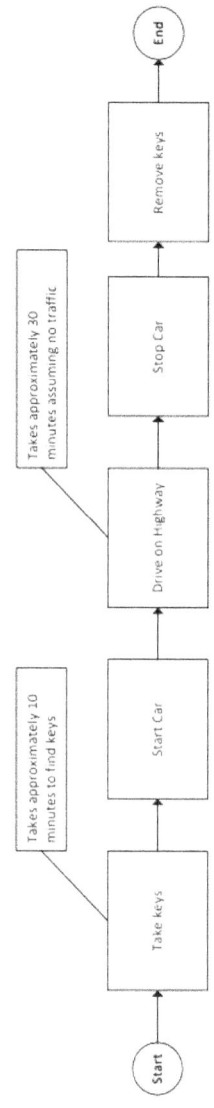

Once data collection is complete, review that as part of your Future State analysis and incorporate those in your recommendations. Your clients may or may not be surprised at the time certain steps take in the process. What is important, however, is that you bring it to their attention. It might be obvious to them but there is a reason they brought in outside counsel for perspective.

Another interesting way to look at data and improvements is by incorporating the Pareto Principle, or the 80/20 rule. In Business Process Improvement speak, this rule states that 20 percent of the actions contribute to 80 percent of the results. Although this is a theory and has been put into practice by a lot of organizations around the world, to wrap your head around it is pretty hard. The book *The 80/20 Principle* by Richard Koch will help you better understand it with the examples provided in the book.[1] I personally have not applied it so far in my career, but am curious and will try to incorporate this either in one of my future projects or in my personal life. It has definitely intrigued me and I would recommend incorporating it in one of your projects, if possible. As you can tell, this surely involves some serious data analysis, so explore it only if you have the luxury to do so.

Summary

1. Data is everywhere, and it's a necessary evil. It is crucial to Business Process Improvement as well.

2. You may not be required to analyze data on your project. Collect it as you conduct your interview process for the Current State document.

3. No fancy tools are required for data collection. Processing time and the time required to review materials should be straightforward.

"Big Data"

4. Analyzing data is for specialists. If the budget and time accommodates, you can either do it yourself if you are qualified and have time, or you can outsource it to someone who is qualified and/or certified.

5. Include annotations in your document to show the time it takes for a certain action or decision. You can also include symbols. For example, add a clock shape to depict the time.

6. Data could be a timestamp or a number, depending on the action. Example for time: time taken to answer the phone. Example for number: number of documents reviewed by a single team.

CHAPTER 8:
REAL-WORLD EXAMPLE

Your preparation for the real world is not in the answers you've learned, but in the questions you've learned how to ask yourself.

—Rainer Maria Rilke

You now have all the knowledge and everything at your disposal to tackle a process flow. Here's a quick overview of what we have covered so far:

Chapter 1: Your mindset and attitude.

Chapter 2: All the basics, including shapes, where to use them, and how to use them.

Chapter 3: We are all creative, so don't overthink it.

Chapter 4: How to set up and conduct an interview. How to engage your audience, and how to gather information for Current State documentation.

Chapter 5: All the phases you go through, including quality checks as you complete your Current State document.

Chapter 6: How to think about and identify improvements for your Future State document.

Chapter 7: How to collect data, if and why you should collect data, and whether or not you should analyze it, either by yourself or with someone else.

With all this knowledge you have amassed, you are now ready to look at something more complex than all the examples you have seen thus far. Remember what I said about process flows and data? It can be simple or complex, depending on the organization or department that you will be looking at. I used an example that is universally understood and complex enough where it goes to two pages to showcase all the shapes that we discussed so far. Hopefully, this gives you a good understanding of everything I've covered and gives you a taste of what it will look like once you begin creating your own documents. I'm no data expert, which is why you will see that I have deliberately omitted data collection and analysis from the example. I encourage you to do that on your own, where you can be the interviewer and interviewee in this case. Have fun with it.

Let's take a look at a process that is more business-focused and something you might encounter either within a small business or a larger organization. For the sake of understanding, I will use an example of today's health care scenario where a member calls their health care insurer to schedule an appointment with their doctor. I have kept the names of the process flows as simple as possible for illustration purposes. However, that's not how they will be named in the business world.

This example is solely to present a real-world scenario; therefore, I have taken a few liberties with the details. If you don't catch everything at first, I will list out the key points so there is no confusion. I have also included my hand-drawn pictures as an example to show how ugly my process flows look when I am sketching them out. But don't let my doodles confuse you. The final output in Visio is where it shines, and *that's* what matters.

List of Assumptions Made for the Current State:

- Member has insurance through this particular health plan.
- Health plan can help with scheduling appointments.
- Health plan has issued an ID card that has their phone number on it.
- Health plan's customer service can assist with scheduling appointments.
- The doctor is in network and accepts this particular insurance.
- Future State is a bit more flexible because a lot of it is built based on Current State.
- Recommendations are provided. However, not every recommendation will be implemented. These are based on best practices, industry standards, and the like. They may not be applicable in all scenarios, so use your judgment when presenting them.

Recommendations can fall into one of the following four categories:

1. **Resources:** To reduce time for a certain action, it may be recommended to add another resource or a team.

2. **System:** To improve customer experience, a new system might be recommended to be implemented.

3. **Training:** Sometimes it can be as simple as changing the order of certain steps or revisiting the existing documentation or policies to change what has always been

in place. Retraining existing resources involves minimal time and capital and can be quickly implemented.

4. **Material:** Creation of specific documentation to help educate internal or external parties either via print or electronic communication.

When capital is involved, the department and/or organization will usually have to go through a set of steps to determine if there is an ROI (Return on Investment) and if there is budget to support that recommendation. That exercise will be outside of the scope of your process improvement initiative, but it is something you can help with after the completion of your current project.

Below are some of the liberties I took for my example of a health care member calling their insurer or health plan to schedule an appointment with their doctor:

- *Scheduling Appointment* and *Meeting Doctor* are two distinct and totally separate processes. However, you will notice I used on-page and off-page connectors, as they are on different pages.
- The numbering for the second process should be independent of the first process and should begin from number one, but I continued it as if it were part of the first process.
- Number sequence does not exactly follow the happy/critical path.
- Space in the file has not been utilized like it should have been. For example, the swim lanes can be longer to accommodate more shapes.

Now since these are example files and the majority of the work has been done (you're welcome), go ahead and play around with the shapes and numbers. Adjust swim lanes, change text in the actions/decisions, and move shapes while avoiding overlapping arrows. If you're feeling adventurous, try to fit two pages in one. There is no limit to what you can do. Don't like the straight arrows? Go for curved ones and see what that looks like. In my experience, creativity becomes exponential when resources are limited. So go ahead, GET CREATIVE!

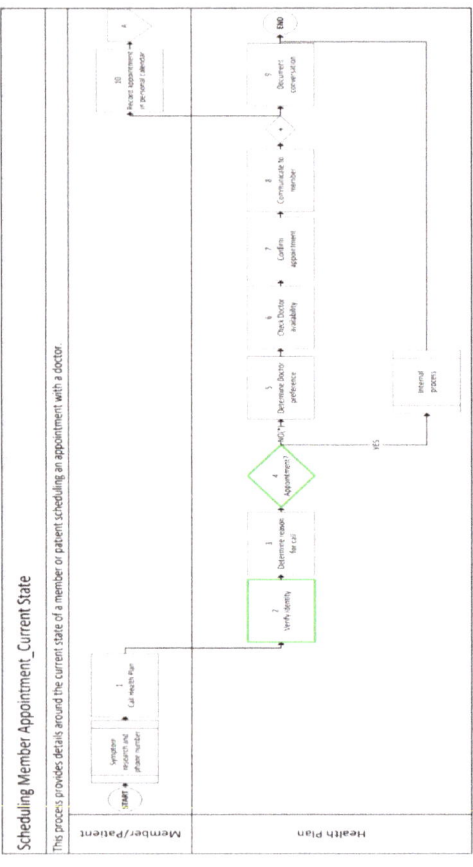

Scheduling Member Appointment_Current State

Real-World Example

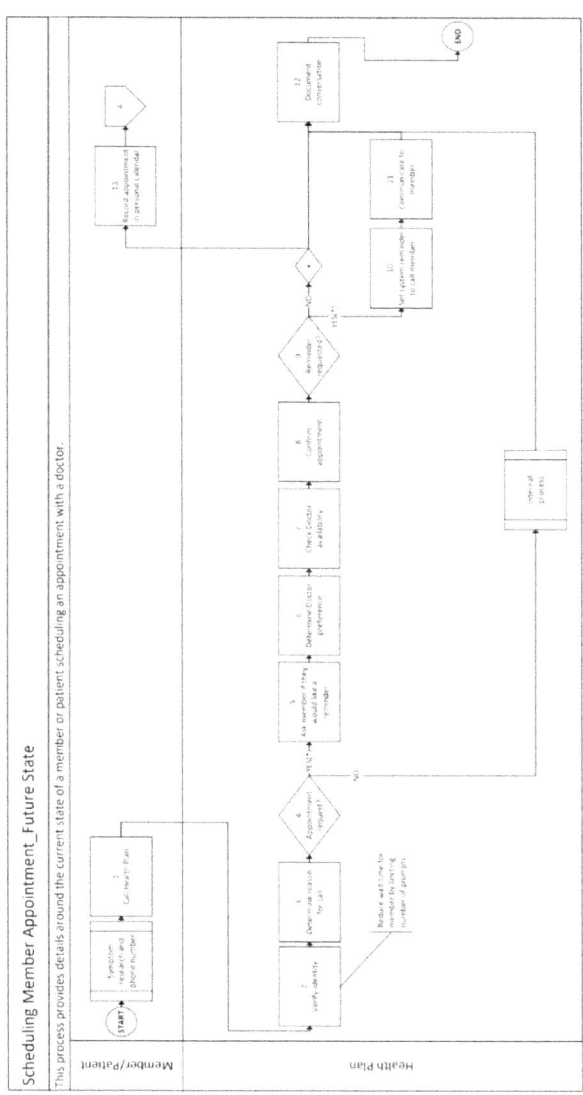

Scheduling Appointment_Future State

Business Process Improvement

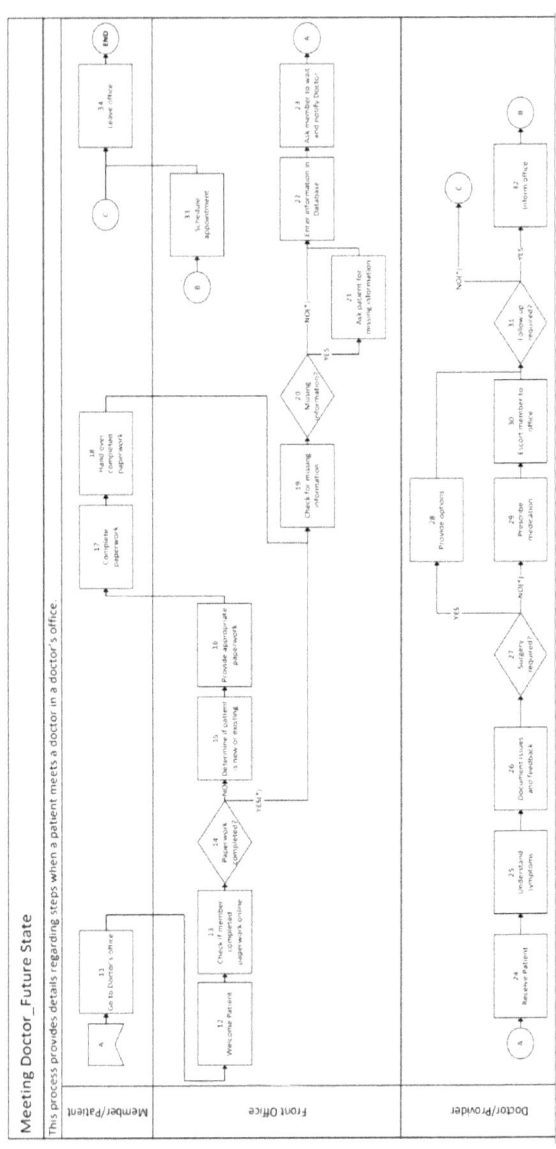

Meeting Doctor_Future State

Real-World Example

Here are the images to the accompanying Current State process flows.

Activity/Process	Description	Duration	Observations for Improvement/Optimization
1 Call Health Plan	Member looks up phone number on the back of their identification card and calls the Health Plan using their landphone for scheduling appointment.	About 10 minutes	It is easy for members to find the phone number. Either available on the card or through their app.
2 Verify Identity	Representative verifies member has said Health Plan's insurance and is an active member	About 5 minutes	Representative has access to the appropriate systems to determine member's eligibility and benefits. Members have to press six prompts and wait for 5 minutes to speak to a representative
3 Determine reason for call	Representative confirms reason for call so they can determine if they can help the member or transfer them to the appropriate department	About 2 minutes	Confirmation is good in this case to truly understand if member was calling for an appointment or they pushed a number to get through
4 Appointment	At this point, representative has to determine if they can handle the call and have the appropriate system handy to help the member	About 2 minutes	Opportunity to provide member with an option to either get a call/email/text message a day or two prior to the appointment. Another opportunity would be to ask the member if they can go to the appointment or if they require assistance.
5 Determine doctor preference	Representative asks member if they want an appointment with a specific doctor or if they received a referral.	About 2 minutes	Asking the member if they have a preference for a doctor is good practice. Representatives can quickly search for the doctor and reduce member's wait time on the phone.

Scheduling Appointment Meeting Doctor

Scheduling Appointment_Current State

Business Process Improvement

#	Action/Decision	Description	Duration	Suggestions for Improvement/optimization
11	Go to Doctor's office	Member makes arrangements to go to the doctor's office on time	Depends on distance	N/A
12	Welcome Patient	Front office welcomes patient	Depends on waiting time	N/A
13	New Patient	Front office determines if this is a first time patient or someone who has a record within their database	About 2 minutes	The Front office has an opportunity to call a member as soon as an appointment is scheduled so they can have the paperwork ready when patient arrives the office
14	Provide new patient paperwork	If it is a new patient, an additional set of paperwork that includes Health Insurance information is required	About 2 minutes	N/A
15	Complete paperwork	Member completes the required paperwork that includes family history, current and old medications	About 10 minutes	The Front office has an opportunity to improve this process by sending a patient an email/text message to complete this information prior to coming into the office

Scheduling Appointment | Meeting Doctor

Meeting Doctor_Future State

Real-World Example

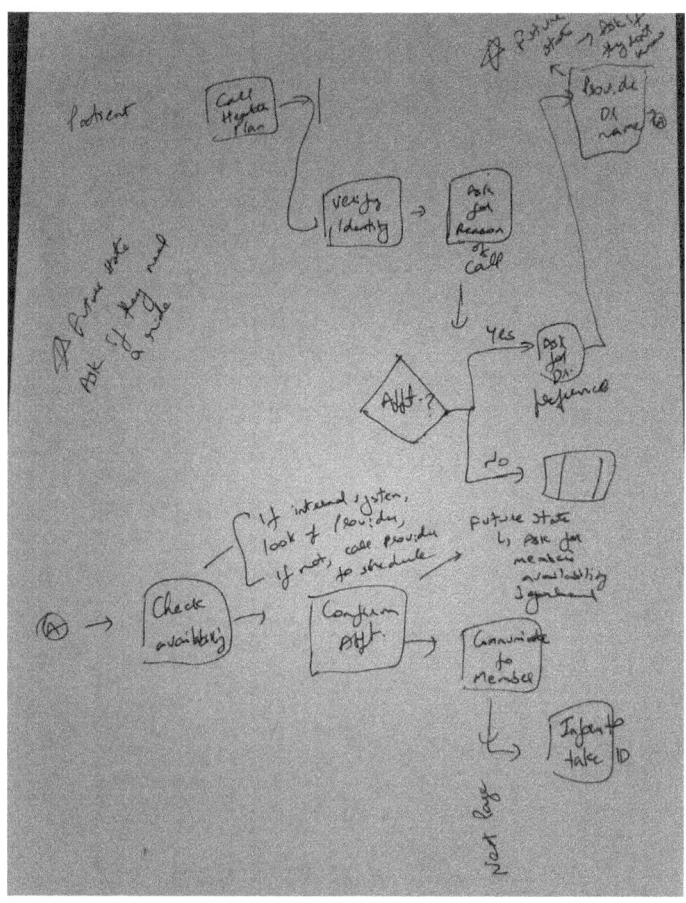

Scheduling Appointment_Current State (hand-drawn)

Business Process Improvement

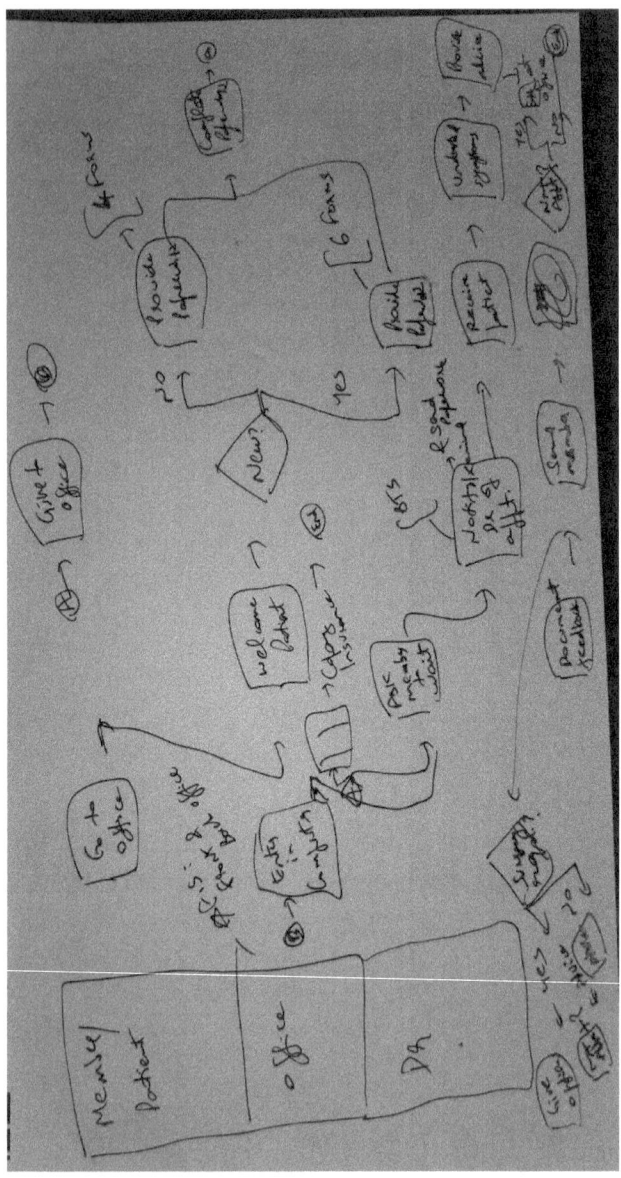

Meeting Doctor_Current State (hand-drawn)

CHAPTER 9:
LAYERS

Everything and everyone has layers. They peel back and present themselves based on the situation.
—Unknown

Presentations get a bad rap. Everyone thinks they are boring, long, drawn-out, and a waste of time. There are multiple books and courses that teach you how to create them with or without using PowerPoint. There are fancy applications out there that try to sell you on why they are better. Personally, I have not seen how they work and have never heard of anyone using them, from my experience. Are they a gimmick? I don't know. Do they really work? I don't know.

All I have experienced in my life is "death by slides." Got a nice ring to it, like "death by chocolate," don't you think? I may have picked this up in one of my jobs and it stuck with me. I have seen leaders try to write books within slides. I have seen some focus on the important parts. I have seen some rely on pictures, graphs, and text, and there are some that tell a story. Everyone has their own reasons on why they chose a specific format and why they feel it is the best way to do it.

Which one of these is my personal favorite? One that tells a story.

Regardless of how you feel about PowerPoint, you will not be using it in this instance. We went through a ton of documentation so far. Did you see PowerPoint as an absolute necessity anywhere? No. Was it deliberate or did the need for it not arise? You must have seen memes or articles or videos about how Jeff Bezos does not want slides in meetings and uses the time to read a summary instead. Or how Elon Musk only gets booked for ten-minute meetings. If the business owners of billion-dollar organizations don't want death by slides, what does that tell you about them? These people value time because that's the most valuable thing to them. They would rather focus their energies on something else. Why try hard and spend so much time on creating documentation when there are bigger fish to fry?

Take a minute to think about all the documentation you have seen in your experience and how much of it could have been avoided. Slides upon slides to convey a single message. It's time that could have been used to rest, relax, or get away from the computer for a while. So this leads me to . . .

Visio. Yes, you can (re)use the process flows you created as your "Presentation." You can tell a story, you can convey your thoughts, you can show pictures—you get the idea.

This is why I love this tool and this area in general. Visio lets you express yourself without being restricted to slides, forcing you to create images, worrying about a format, struggling to find the perfect template, arguing with others on what shapes or colors to use, deciding whether or not animations are necessary, choosing what pictures are most effective, calculating how much text is too much text . . . whew!

The beauty of a Future State process flow is that you can simply reuse your existing process flow document to tell your story, your way. Highlight what is important to the end user and drive focus to the point you want to draw their attention to, without someone in the audience worrying about whether or not you have a typo in some insignificant shape or letting someone sidetrack the conversation in a direction that is neither helpful nor important.

Imagine a direct, focused meeting where all participants are engaged. You get the outcome you need without unnecessary distractions. Visio helps you with that, which is why you must have layers in your arsenal. There might be instances where you are required to use PowerPoint, but try to avoid using it when you can. If you hear, "We have always used PowerPoint," or "We have not used Visio to present before," then your eyes should light up and you should take this opportunity to create a prototype (theoretically speaking) and present it. What is the worst case here anyway? So without further ado, let's take a look.

Call it a gimmick or a fancy presentation technique, but everyone loves a 3D projection. We can do something similar that "pops" off the screen to enhance a process or a step that requires attention. I have used this in the past, and it does elicit a decent response. Frankly, I love it when the specific process or step pops on the screen and makes it easier to read when doing a presentation.

It is not that complicated, and this is an optional step. Feel free to skip this section if you like.

So you already have the key item that you require for your presentation: your Future State process map. Remember, this is where all your recommendations are. Now take a look at all the shapes where you are recommending either an improvement or something that is great. You are telling a story here, so it's not just about negatives or opportunities. You can also talk about something that is really good or stands out in a positive way. This can be something similar along the lines of an activity that is currently on par with a best practice in the industry.

We already saw how to color code them, so let's see how we can play with layers.

Select the shapes you want to highlight and assign them to a layer by going to the ribbon and selecting the "Layer" option. To do this, hold Ctrl and click all the shapes that either have green or are important to understand from a context standpoint.

Just a few detailed steps here for those that are new or need a refresher on how to do this in Visio.

After assigning shapes to a layer, go into the "Layers" option in the ribbon and select "Layer Properties." When you are presenting, simply uncheck the "Visible" box for all the layers, except for the layer you just created for presentation purposes. You will see that the shapes you selected will be the only ones that remain visible on your document.

There are a couple of options you can choose for selecting a layer to present.

1. Only the shape
2. The Critical/Happy path

Let me elaborate.

If you choose option #1, you might have to do a bit more explaining during your presentation, since context is key to why you are displaying that particular shape.

If you choose option #2, your audience will see what you want to focus on without having the need to explain the entire thought process on how a decision was made on highlighting a box where a change is being recommended. Also, if you choose option #2, select the arrows as well to assign to the layer you wish to present. This will ensure that the flow does not get disrupted. Otherwise your actions/decisions will look like they are suspended in the air with no connectivity. That will not look pretty and will leave your audience confused.

That's it! When you are presenting and want to focus on the specific layer, select the layer and go back to presentation mode.

Presentation Mode: Just like any Microsoft Office software, when presenting, it is always a good idea to use the Presentation Mode (full screen). This is a better mode in which your audience will not see the menu on the left. Your process flow fills up the screen and text will be more visible so your audience will not have to squint to read it. Unless, of course, your audience is already familiar with the document.

As always, know your audience and choose which route you want to take. If the audience is very familiar with the process, they don't need it to be explained. For someone who is seeing it for the first time, isolating a shape will confuse them, and you might end up explaining more than you intended to. This will take up valuable time. So know your audience and plan for it. Depending on the process flow, you could decide what you want to focus on and how you want to present.

Now, depending on what you want to show or hide, you can check the appropriate box, and the shapes will appear or disappear on the screen based on your selection.

Assigning Shapes: I would leave the defaults alone. When I create my new layer, I click "New" within the sub-menu and name the layer "Presentation" so I know exactly which one to go for when I am presenting. By doing so, I'm not figuring out what I had named it. So don't be ambiguous when you name your layer. This will save you some frustration. So plan ahead.

On a last note, you can also rename a layer instead of using the default Layer 1, Layer 2, etc. When you are switching during a presentation, your audience will see what you named them. If you choose the standard default option, it will not come across as professional. These are some things that may or may not make a difference to your audience. But these little things are what separate you from the rest. Plus, we don't want to come across as lazy now, do we?

After the presentation is complete, ensure you get physical signatures (if that is a requirement for your project) on your Future State process flows.

Summary

1. Layers are a fun way to create a "pop" during a presentation.

2. Decide if you want to highlight just one shape or the entire path.

3. Rename layers so they look professional when presenting the document to your audience.

CHAPTER 10:
IMPROVE

Perfection does not exist. You can always do better and you can always grow.
—Les Brown

The definition of *improve* is "to enhance in value or quality: make better."[1] Whether in our professional or personal life, we should always try to better ourselves. Imagine if we didn't go on a quest to improve as a species, then we would have been nomads hunting for food and eating whatever we could, living in the wild. Refinement and learned efficiency is what makes us stand apart from other species. Continuously improving ourselves also sets us apart from others and makes us stand out from the competition. You have already taken that step toward betterment by investing in your educating and/or improving your knowledge of Business Processes Improvement by picking up this book. So congratulations on taking the first step!

Pat yourself on the back a little. In the journey of this book, you went from knowing nothing about process flows to creating one on your own! You have improved on your knowledge and are now ready to impart your wisdom to others. Since you are here, don't rest on your laurels because you still have work to do. Enjoy the success and outcomes you had in presenting your Future State documentation, but look toward how you can improve even more, specifically analyzing how you went about the project.

Think you're done? Not so fast. There is one last thing to do before we officially wrap up. You must conduct a Lessons Learned session. It is always a good practice to conduct a Lessons Learned at the end of a project, no matter what type of project it is. This provides insight into all the things you did well and . . . let's face it, all the things you didn't do well. In other words, all the things that could have been done better. Process improvement doesn't get better than that, right?

Just to be clear on the function of Lessons Learned. These are different and entirely separate from the actual project. These "improvements" are related to your approach to the project and completely unrelated to the project you are working on. Examples of Lessons learned could include:

- Interviews were scheduled well in advance. (What went well?)
- All SMEs were not identified at the beginning of the project. (What can be improved?)
- Allocated time of sixty minutes for interview (Round 1) was sufficient. (What went well?)
- Allocated time of thirty minutes for review meeting was not sufficient. (What can be improved?)
- Presentation of process flow was clear to follow along. (What went well?)
- Excel sheet can include more detail. (What can be improved?)

As you can see, these are totally unrelated to the actual process flow you were working on. These are more related to the process you followed. It's not just limited to your approach;

it also includes the approach of the client/sponsor as part of the project (see Example #2).

Tip: Every time you come across a situation where you think, *Oh, this is nice! They are proactive in getting SharePoint access approved*, jot that down in your notes as a positive.

Notes are not limited to meetings. There are things that pop up consciously or subconsciously during a project. And the best part is they are not directly related to the process flow; they sit outside, inviting you to jot them down when you get a thought and then get back to it later.

In this case, you won't be documenting a process flow; instead, it will be a document, which does not have be complicated, so you could use PowerPoint. It can be a simple layout that should capture your essentials: the session/meeting name, a brief description of the meeting, date it occurred, and your initial observations. Don't suggest or document improvements yet. On the day of the meeting to gather feedback, let everyone else provide their input first. Depending on the number of people involved, schedule a one-hour meeting (or less). That should be sufficient time to gather feedback. Everyone will have something positive or negative to provide, and all feedback is good feedback. Negative feedback should not be taken personally, since smoother processes are the desired outcome for all involved. The hope is that everyone and everything improves with the collective feedback.

Scheduling

Ideally, you will be scheduling this within two weeks after the end of the project. Past that timeframe, everyone will forget certain aspects or things they wanted to mention. Unless, of course, there is someone who has a really good memory or is noting things as they go along. It's always surprising after a feedback session as to how people remember tiny bits of detail. I have seen my fair share of these folks (sometimes not in a good way), so consider yourself warned. If you commit to documenting these notes and paying strict attention, all the better. Also, remember that your sole focus is this project and this project only, whereas the client/sponsor is juggling multiple projects. So it'll be rare that someone will be dedicated solely to your project.

Lessons Learned are pretty much self-explanatory, so everyone will understand the subject line when they see an invite in their inbox.

Feel free to use this meeting invite template:

- Subject: Project Name_Lessons Learned_Workshop
- Body: *Thank you for your participation in Project_Name. As part of the wrap up, we would like to invite you to a Lessons Learned workshop to identify opportunities for improvement in the project approach. We appreciate your time.*
- Key sections to include in the Lessons Learned document:

—What went well?

—What can be improved?

Notice how I said *what can be improved* and not *what didn't go well* or *what went bad*? How a feedback statement is viewed is based on one's perception. If you include something in your document that says "bad," it immediately gets all the attention and takes focus away from the "good" that happened on the project. Once people see "bad," they will start thinking about everything that went wrong with the project, forcing you to reorient everyone into thinking and speaking about the positives. Using the word "improved" has a positive air about it and implies the genuine feeling of wanting to improve on things that could have gone a lot better, be it personal interaction, systems, and timing, which allows people to adopt a different approach. You don't want people to be too negative in this meeting; the idea is to understand what could have been better. I am not going to say, "We will solve all the problems here," nor am I implying that your role is to be a problem-solver in this meeting. The goal is to capture all the positives and the opportunities that were found during the course of the project. See what I did there? Okay, I'll stop now.

Key Items to Include

After all feedback is collected, take some time to separate out the negatives and come up with solutions to how some of those items can be improved. Document the recommendations and review those in the following meeting. Ensure all associated parties agree to those recommendations and end the session.

Takeaways for Lessons Learned

- All Current State documents should be stored in the Current State folder.
- All Future State documents should be stored in the Future State folder.
- All documents used for reference should be stored in the reference/archive folder.
- Package them all, and send them in an email, or upload the digital documents in an online repository if access is available.

Summary

1. Continuous improvement makes you stand apart.

2. Lessons Learned from a project will only help you become better and improve your experience on the next project.

3. Schedule meetings while the project is still fresh in everyone's mind.

4. Take all feedback, positive and constructive. It's not personal and will only help you and others moving forward.

5. Be consistent, such as always storing documentation in the appropriate locations.

CHAPTER 11:
WHAT NEXT?

What happens next is up to you.
—Chris Sacca

The definition of next is "adjacent (as in place, rank, or time)."[1] You have closed out the project, learned a few things, and picked up a few skills along the way. Where do you go from here? First, take a step back and reflect. The project is now in your rearview mirror. You went through a lot of emotions and learned a lot. Not just about the topic but about the people involved as well. You may not have realized that you became a Subject Matter Expert yourself. You know everything, not just about the process and its intricacies but the people associated with it too. Now that's definitely an achievement.

In a simplistic sense, there are two ways to go from here.

1. Continue to work on Business Process Improvement projects.

2. Do not work on any Business Process Improvement projects.

I am encouraging you, at this point in your career or phase in life, to reflect on your time in this project. As with everything, look at the pros and cons. Think about what you liked best, then consider your not-so-favorite parts. If you have not worked on a project before and only went through this book to get a sampling, did you enjoy the topic? Did you enjoy the process? Did you understand how it works? Did it excite you to find improvements that may or may not have been obvious initially? Did you have fun playing around, moving shapes, identifying improvements in the documents or the example I provided in Chapter 8?

If you didn't really enjoy it, then maybe this business style is not for you. Depending on the stage you're at in your career, you can either switch careers or find something that motivates you. As you saw throughout the course of this book, these kinds of projects involve interactions with a lot of people, either clients or peers. This demands lots of opinions and learning how to expertly navigate them. It also involves volumes of documentation, including process flows, Excel sheets, and—depending on the project—extreme data analysis. Not to mention you'll likely have a tight timeline and a demanding schedule to meet deadlines for deliverables, which you may not have to plan yourself. Not every project is alike but it is typically how every project would be. Does that deter you or does it excite you?

If you have decided to continue on this path, great! I am going to provide some information for you that you can use to further your career and quench your thirst for more knowledge. If you choose not to continue on this path, that's great too! It is important to know what you like and what you don't like so you can work on and excel in whatever you choose. So if you are ready to continue on this journey, I will advise you on how to proceed next.

If you enjoyed what you learned and were engaged with the interactions, it's a sign you should continue to pursue Business

Process Improvement projects. In order to establish yourself as an authority in any field, it is considered ideal if you acquire a certification. In the next chapter, I have provided options for certifications you can obtain to help you along your journey.

Certification is a tricky subject. If you would like to learn more about the different ways to get certified, I offer the absolute best options available on the market in the next chapter. A quick Web search will inform you that Six Sigma and PMP (Project Management Professional) certifications usually go hand-in-hand for Business Process Improvement. This should come as no surprise to you if you have gone through the earlier chapters. As you know, there is always a an organization that is internationally recognized and considered to be a gold standard. In order to have a certification that is globally recognized, I would highly recommend looking into Six Sigma. This is the most recognizable and highly respected certifying body in the world when it comes to Business Process Improvement. And the best part about it is the certification doesn't expire! Unlike certain certifications that require Continuing Education Credits (CEC) or some kind of learning tasks to complete to keep a certification active, once you receive a Six Sigma certification, you are set for life!

You know what means: You pay for the test once, pass it, and you will not be required to ever pay a fee to maintain it or keep it active. Certified Product Owner certification requires you to pay a fee every two years to keep your certification active. So what more can you ask for? In my opinion, Six Sigma is the best bang for your buck and will serve you well forever. Should you switch careers but ultimately come back to Business Process Improvement, your certification is still valid, and all you have to do is brush up on your concepts and you are ready to roll.

There are a minimum required training hours to be eligible to take the test if you have not worked on a project. If you have real-time experience, you can skip some of the training and become eligible to take the test. Requirements for the exam change every so often, so take time to review them or ask the organization of your choice for the latest requirements for test eligibility.

Wherever you are located in the world, you should be able to find a local or a remote organization that is authorized by Six Sigma to be able to take the test. They will assess where you are, walk you through the requirements, and determine if you need additional training or if your experience satisfies the requirements. Once that is cleared, you are ready to begin your certification.

So is certification absolutely necessary, or will experience be enough? Let me do a quick summary of the pros and cons here and let you make that decision.

Certification

Having a piece of paper that shows you intentionally chose to learn, engage, and stretch your skills will definitely lend you some credibility. It means you have learned the core concepts and demonstrated the ability to implement those concepts in the real world. That is definitely worth pursuing. Think about it: You know how it should work, even though it may be completely different from how it works in the real world. When you are confronted with a situation, use your creativity and come up with solutions to help tackle it. Also, you would not be completely new to the situation. You probably came up with all sorts of issues when you were working on your project for the certification. So is not having experience really a big problem? If I have to categorize what you will achieve by getting a certification, here are the three main gains:

1. **Credibility:** Nothing speaks more than having a certification attached to your name. It means you have worked hard, learned concepts, and passed a test.

2. **Concepts:** Acquiring skills and challenging yourself shows that you understand what is required of the role or position.

3. **Soft Skill:** A certificate demonstrates the desire to learn and put in the effort to completion. This may seem like a soft argument, but think about it. You went out of your way to learn something new and accomplished it. If that doesn't show your drive to learn new things and do better in a role or position that is along the same lines, then what else will?

These are important points to consider and use when you are applying for a position that aligns with your interests. Becoming certified in this niche will likely pay in dividends, especially when you are seeking internal opportunities. On the flip side, it doesn't really help you with getting external opportunities unless you have real-time experience (at least in my case). Unless you have proven yourself helpful within an organization, your certification may not really hold a lot of value.

Experience

You are aware of the vicious circle: no job equals no experience. But how would you gain experience without getting a job? However, if someone was willing to give you an opportunity, it's important to grab it. Nothing beats real-world experience. It gives you a chance to experience personal interactions, feedback, real-time pressure, and allows you get better at your craft.

If you have attended interviews with consulting firms such Bain, Accenture, Deloitte, or E&Y in the past or are preparing for one, you should be aware that part of the interview process includes case studies. For the uninitiated, this is where a case study of an organization is provided, usually depicting a scenario of a decision they made at a certain point in time. You, the interviewee, would be asked to read the case study, analyze it, then prepare to offer your perspective of the situation. There are no right or wrong answers, as no one has a crystal ball to predict the future. What is being assessed, however, is your understanding of the situation and whether or not you can offer a comprehensive overview on whatever your stance is. This interview line serves a purpose to understand your critical-thinking analysis when you are asked to come up with a solution to a business problem faced by a client.

However, when it comes to interviewing for Business Process Improvement, I am not aware of an interviewer asking an interviewee to map out Current State and Future State process flow documents. Things may have changed in the recent past, and I may not be aware, but depending on the number of interview rounds and how long an interview is scheduled for, things might be different. You could compare this to interviews by tech companies for software engineer positions where an interviewee is asked to write a few lines of code to demonstrate their knowledge in that space. If you are certified, however, all of this is moot since you have displayed successfully that you are well-versed in the concepts.

Regardless, as you continue working on these projects, you will start to pick up on and learn invaluable things as you continue through this journey. I would highly recommend preparing for and getting a certification. There are multiple advantages in getting a certification. Some of them being:

- Reinforcement of core concepts
- Learning new concepts and techniques
- Recognition of having specialized skill set

- Employment or project opportunities

Keep in mind that learning never ends. I would highly recommend joining groups on LinkedIn where ideas are shared and questions are asked. Being involved on platforms such as these keep your skills sharpened and offers a fresh perspective when someone provides a solution that is atypical.

What's next for me, you ask? Since I finally published this book, I want to create a course for Business Process Improvement and post it on various MOOC (Massive Online Open Courses) platforms, such as Coursera, LinkedIn, and Udemy.

Summary

1. Take time to reflect on your assigned project. Identify both the good and the problematic parts of the project.

2. Decide if you want to continue on this path of career of Business Process Improvement.

3. Certification shows you are well-versed in the concepts and can execute Business Process Improvement within any industry.

4. The Business Process Improvement is industry agnostic; that's why there is one certification for them all.

5. Getting a certification from Six Sigma is a good investment for your personal and career life.

6. Certification > Experience? Tough to say. It varies from organization to organization and from person to person.

CHAPTER 12:
SIX SIGMA AND CMMI

Perception is reality. If you are perceived to be something, you might as well be it because that's the truth in people's minds.

—Steve Young

As I mentioned in the previous chapter, certification plays a big part in how people perceive you. Perception is reality! How others perceive us and our reputation matters, especially in business.[1]

Since I have waxed eloquent about Six Sigma, I want to provide you with the basics so you can understand and appreciate the fundamentals of the concept. I will also provide brief descriptions of the available certifications under Six Sigma and give you an overview of an alternate organization called CMMI, which is similar but different compared to Six Sigma. CMMI focuses on Business Process Improvement as well, but the major focus is on the overall organization—not just from an internal department perspective. Again, these are the most popular options available, and you can choose to pursue whichever method makes the most sense to you. If you want to know which certification I lean toward, I am biased because

I am Six Sigma certified. Plus, it continues to be a more popular program compared to CMMI.

Since this is a primer, I would be remiss if this book did not include basic Six Sigma and CMMI principles to continue your Business Process Improvement journey. These the fundamentals are being included so you can get familiar with the terminology can plan which certification you choose to pursue.

Six Sigma

Six Sigma is a methodology that is now synonymous with Process Improvement. The goal of this methodology is that everything can be measured and improved based on a certain tool set. As someone who has achieved one of their certifications, I can definitely say there is some truth to that. It can largely work, if you stay true to the principles and tool set, depending on the circumstances.

There are varying levels of certification you can aspire to, depending on where you are in your journey. Certified professionals achieve "Belts." These can be compared to the belts achieved in Karate or Taekwondo. The various certifications you can receive in order of mastery are:

1. **Six Sigma Yellow Belt:** someone who understands Six Sigma principles and can assist in a Six Sigma project

2. **Six Sigma Green Belt:** someone who can actively participate in Six Sigma projects and help with documentation and analysis

3. **Six Sigma Black Belt:** someone who can lead Six Sigma projects and coach teammates

4. **Six Sigma Master Black Belt:** someone who can train and coach Black Belts, essentially providing expertise

As you can see, Six Sigma Master Black is the highest belt you can receive. Though White and Brown Belts are an option for beginners, they are not desirable since they don't require Six Sigma projects for completion. If you really want to obtain a certification, go for Yellow or above. Keep in mind that requirements for achieving these certifications include passing a test and/or submitting a project that satisfies all of the principles. There are other variations with Six Sigma, such as Lean Six Sigma, but the fundamentals are the same.

For more information, you can go to their website: https://asq.org/quality-resources/six-sigma.[2]

Six Sigma consists of six essential principles that are rolled up into one abbreviation: DMAIC. If you have read all of the chapters above, most of these will sound very familiar.

1. **Define:** This is where the project scope is defined, including what outcome you wish from the project. It could be reduction in time, improvement in performance (either physical or emotional), or an increase in savings. It is also important to include what you would *not* be covering as part of the project. The list of required activities here include:

- Project Charter
- Deliverable List
- Project Plan (including schedule)

2. **Measure:** This is where interviews are conducted, AS-IS process flows are created and approval is received for the Current State. The list of required activities here include:

- Workshops/Interviews
- AS-IS process flow (Current State)

3. **Analyze:** This is where the complete data captured in the "Measure" phase is thoroughly reviewed and opportunities for improvement are identified. It goes without saying that this is the most critical phase. The list of required activities here include:

- Review AS-IS data
- Create TO-BE process flow (Future State)

4. **Improve:** This is where all recommendations are agreed upon and officially signed off. The list of required activities here include:

- Build Solution
- Test Solution

5. **Control:** This is where the solution is implemented. The list of required activities here include:

- Implementation
- Analyze Results

CMMI

CMMI stands for Capability Maturity Model Integration. While Six Sigma is focused on projects, CMMI is focused more on the organization. (20,000-foot view vs. 100-foot view).

CMMI has five Maturity Levels that indicate what state the organization is in. The Maturity Levels can also be used to determine the state of a specific department since these principles are applicable there too. Here are the five levels:

- **Level 1:** In this stage, the organization is either fairly new or struggles with sudden growth. There is little, if any, documentation, and there is confusion on how to get the processes organized.

- **Level 2:** In this stage, the organization has resources assigned while still requiring some documentation. However, there is still a lot of stress for the wrong reasons surrounding accountability, processes, and documentation.

- **Level 3:** In this stage, the organization has achieved some sort of stability around resources and their documentation. They have a process, but left alone, they can get the job done.

- **Level 4:** In this stage, the organization performs at a high level and continues to improve and work on shortcomings around their documentation and processes.

- **Level 5:** The organization is performing at the highest level. Everything has been defined, including the everyday work and the opportunities to further excel.[3]

As you can see, the goal for every organization would be to get to Level 5 because that is the ultimate, high-performing, well-oiled machine. To simplify what it means to be a Level 5, it means there is no re-work/duplication, no confusion on assignments, no confusion around expectations, no documentation issues or questions. The quality of the end products is high, and having clearly defined processes ensures cost is kept as low as possible. For any type of organization (for-profit or non-profit organizations), this is ideal because the end customer they are serving will benefit from your expertise.

Final words on certification:

I feel it is invaluable in itself. If you get a certification, it means you have demonstrated discipline and put in the effort to learn the concepts. You've also applied them in scenarios where you have showcased the improvements in whatever business process you have chosen.

If you are a job-seeker looking for opportunities, a quick look at the certification section of the job description will pique your interest. There will be jobs that require a certification, and there will be jobs that will note that a certification is preferred. If you are already armed with one, you will be smiling because you know you qualify for both scenarios. You will definitely stand out when a certification is a preferred requirement. Now you get to choose which opportunity works better for you, and then start narrowing down the companies you want to work for.

So you see, your chances of landing a better job dramatically improve by obtaining one or both of these certifications! If you look at the salary ranges, you can negotiate toward the higher salary based on your certification. That in itself puts you in a better negotiating position.

A quick look at the current job descriptions (and the market is *hot* at the time of writing this) and you will see that the starting annual salary in the United States for a Process Improvement Analyst (entry level) is between $65–$70K. This is a rough estimate, as organizations don't share the salary range in general. However, the amount could definitely be higher based on inflation and other factors. Understand that having a certification can help you because you'll have the leverage. For those with no experience, don't be disheartened. Some organizations may even accept a certification in lieu of experience, so that will work in your favor.

A quick note: Process Improvement Analyst is the technical term. However, some organizations will have these titles listed as Business Analyst. Take a look at the job description to determine what the organization is looking for. Remember, analysis is a big component of process improvement, and titles are based on company rules.

Summary

1. Six Sigma is a universally recognized certifying body.

2. Get certified based on where you are in your Process Improvement journey.

3. CMMI focuses on maturity of organizations and classifies them into five levels.

4. Six Sigma is process-focused while CMMI is organization-focused. Take some time to research both of these organizations, then decide which one makes sense for you.

5. Don't overthink. Pick one and immerse yourself with the training!

CONCLUSION

So there you have it. The wild journey of Business Process Improvement seen through my eyes—and now through yours. There were a lot of "how-tos" that I covered, but hopefully this book answered some or all of your questions. Thank you for sticking with me, and congrats on completing it if you went through all the chapters! Whether this book increased your understanding of the concepts or increased your knowledge of business savviness in general, I hope you came out wiser than before you started reading it.

There are two important takeaways that I cannot stress enough: focusing your mindset and enjoying the journey. At the end of the day, it really boils down to how much of the advice you have taken to heart and how much of it you devote yourself to. Choose wisely, my friend!

Mindset: Be clear on what you want to achieve. There are multiple ways to achieve a goal, and only you can decide how you want to go about achieving it. Work hard? Work smart? How about you start by working hard, and in due course you will end up working smart. How is that accomplished? By improving yourself and improving everything you do . . . one action at a time. I'm certain you've heard "You can do anything you set your mind to." It's a true statement. To activate your intentions, all you have to do is set a goal, create a path to get there, and then take action to achieve it! The best way to achieve something is to take that first, uncertain step, then watch everything fall into place when you allow momentum and confidence to fuel your journey.

Journey: There's no point in doing something you don't enjoy, so why not enjoy the journey? It isn't easy to put blinders on and only focus on the end goal. You can learn a lot with every interaction—be it with people, organizations, and even yourself. You will gain a higher understanding of yourself as you interact with and react to new situations and new people, but it requires flexibility and open-mindedness. You will be surprised to see how much life has to offer when you start noticing and observing things and human beings. If an opportunity presents itself to be a fly on the wall for certain important meetings, go ahead and listen in. Everything is a learning experience, so don't hesitate when presented with an opportunity. Fear of failure prevents a lot of people from achieving their full potential, so don't make the mistake of never putting yourself out there.

If you have paid close attention, I gave you a couple of different examples in this book for putting the processes into action. One was a daily, routine chore of driving to the office and/or grocery store. The other was in a business setting as described in Chapter 8. It was a bit deliberate to show you that Business Process Improvement is not limited to your professional life. It can be used in exactly the same way in your personal life as well. It is easy to look at the outside world and show others what they are doing wrong and what actions they need to take to improve their life or process. But if someone gave you the same advice about how you go about living your life, you would think that's rude and mean, right? Maybe you would even think it's none of their business.

If you want to better yourself, you should have checkpoints and touchpoints for your personal goals as well. There is a reason why coaches exist; they are there to watch you from the outside and give advice to help you improve. Think of coaches either for fitness, academia, or sports. Having a coach keeps you accountable and only has your best interest at heart. They keep you motivated and help you celebrate major milestones. Wishing for things does not work. You have to put in the work and effort to achieve whatever you wish for.

Let's now recap Business Process Improvement in a business setting. All of the shapes, and their descriptions and usage, only serve as a starting point to help you get what you want. The more you practice, the better you will get and the more confident you will be. If you don't have work experience, you can easily pick up a process that you see from your life and create documentation to show why something is not working and how it can be improved. Don't sit back and wait for things to fall into your lap. Get up and make things happen.

Like you have seen, there are no complicated tools required to document and show improvements to a process. Same thing is true with data analysis, if you selected a process to practice and work on. Remember, we are all creative, so if you don't find something worthwhile, then make up a process. Think of the things that can go wrong and show how it can be improved. There is nothing limiting you, so why not at least do some practice work. Time to get cracking!

Network and you will find like-minded people who would be willing to work with you and act as a reviewer to go through the "phases." They might provide some great insight as you slowly move toward the Future State. With this experience, you will continue to grow not just professionally but personally as well.

The goal is to get better, and when you follow an organized system, you will improve. Certification will only serve as icing on the cake if you enjoy what you are doing. Analysis-paralysis is a real thing. So don't over-analyze what you should be doing. You are a Business Process Improvement expert now. If you find something is going off track, you know that you have to course-correct and will continue doing exceptional things. Challenge yourself to a project of your own. There is nothing better than working on something you initiated and learning and discovering things as you go along.

So go ahead and find something that bothers you in your daily life. This could be an interaction at a bank, utilities company, or a grocery store. Or, if you want to bring about a change in your workplace because you feel things could be better, start documenting the Current State. The most important thing here is to not get distracted by life. Set a realistic start and end date for your project. Nothing too short and nothing too long. Space it out just enough using the general rules I provided in the chapters to come up with a realistic timeline. Try not to get distracted with activities outside your control, and then begin working. Who knows, once your project is complete, you can show it to your supervisor or manager and might end up getting the job you wanted! Even if it doesn't go anywhere, it's okay. You're a much different person now and have gained an incredible amount of knowledge. If you don't get encouragement, appreciation, and recommendations and instead get reprimanded, this is a sure sign that you should find a new job. You know what they say about knowledge: no one can steal it from you.

Remember, what I shared with you is my experience only. Someone in the same scenario as me would have viewed this differently and probably has their own take on it. Every organization is different, and every project is different. Everything that I have learned and everyone that I have interacted with will likely be vastly different from what you are going to experience. The important points to take away are the basics found

Conclusion

in these pages, plus maintaining a positive mindset, provided you are motivated and interested in the topic.

So go ahead and work on a project you can call your own. You can find me on LinkedIn, and I will try to help in any way I can. Sharpen those pencils and start creating some documents. Let's change the world one process flow at a time!

NOTES

Chapter 1: Mindset

1. Malcolm Gladwell, *Outliers: The Story of Success* (Bay Back Books, 2011).

2. Leslie Bradshaw, "Big Data and What It Means," U.S. Chamber of Commerce Foundation, https://www.uschamberfoundation.org/bhq/big-data-and-what-it-means.

Chapter 2: Basics

1. Definition of "swim lane," Standards Development Organization, https://www.bpmn.org.

2. Definition of "action," Merriam Webster's Online Dictionary, https://www.merriam-webster.com/dictionary/action.

3. Definition of "corroborate," Online Cambridge English Dictionary, https://dictionary.cambridge.org/us/dictionary/english/corroborate.

Chapter 3: Creativity

1. Definition of "creativity," Lexico, https://www.lexico.com/en/definition/creativity.

2. Definition of "manipulation," Lexico, https://www.lexico.com/en/definition/manipulation.

Chapter 4: Current State

1. Definition of "current," Merriam Webster's Online Dictionary, https://www.merriam-webster.com/dictionary/current.

Chapter 5: Phases

1. Definition of "phase," Merriam Webster's Online Dictionary, https://www.merriam-webster.com/dictionary/phase.

Chapter 6: Future State

1. Definition of "future state," Merriam Webster's Online Dictionary, https://www.merriam-webster.com/dictionary/future.

Chapter 7: "Big Data"

1. Richard Koch, *The 80/20 Principle: The Secret to Achieving More with Less* (Crown Business, 1997).

Chapter 10: Improve

1. Definition of "improve," Merriam Webster's Online Dictionary, https://www.merriam-webster.com/dictionary/improve.

Chapter 11: What's Next?

1. Definition of "next," Merriam Webster's Online Dictionary, https://www.merriam-webster.com/dictionary/next.

Chapter 12: Six Sigma and CMMI

1. Steve Stauning, "Perception Is Everything," Ask the Manager blog, https://askthemanager.com/2019/06/perception-is-everything/#.YrpAVi-B1mA.

2. "What Is Six Sigma," ASQ, https://asq.org/quality-resources/six-sigma.

3. Stephen Watts, "CCMI: An Introduction to Capability Maturity Model Integration," BmcBlogs,https://www.bmc.com/blogs/cmmi-capability-maturity-model-integration/.

ACKNOWLEDGMENTS

Eric Dahlem—For bringing me into a different department within the organization I was working for. Thank you for your leadership.

Shrey Sekhar—For instilling confidence in me, taking me under your wing, and helping me see the bigger picture and think beyond a process flow. Thank you, Shrey!

Reno Fiedler—For teaching me the art and science behind creating a process flow. Being from Germany, he knows a thing or two about structure, and definitely about science. Thanks, Reno.

Chris Miladinovich – For being a fantastic mentor and getting me initiated on the path to progress

Jenna Love—For patiently working with me on my first book. Her guidance and help in getting my message across so eloquently is much appreciated. Thank you for your work.

Barry Lyons – My proofreader extraordinaire who patiently read through and provided vital feedback. Thank you!

Lance Buckley – For helping design a fantastic cover. Super excited with his process and what he was able to create for me with the little information I gave him.Thank you and thanks to Bridget!

ABOUT THE AUTHOR

Sai Gudlavalleti was born and raised in Western and Southern India. He was such a voracious reader while growing up that he would read anything and everything he possibly could, but he loved fiction as a child the most. The low-light reading conditions he endured were all self-induced because he was supposed to be sleeping, so he relied on weak light sources to make sure no one noticed he was awake. These sneaky childhood episodes ended in him needing slight vision correction at an early age! With a renewed interest in reading nonfiction later in life, he continues to read and listen to audiobooks. His interest in expanding his knowledge has led to him to the roles of consultant, project manager, program manager, and a certified product owner. He lives with his wife and son in Atlanta, Georgia.

Fun fact: After a decade or more of missing out on the playful side of life due to his work-life schedule getting off balance, Gudlavalleti now makes time for the activities he enjoys, such as playing the occasional video game on his PlayStation and being an RPG (Role-Playing Games) fan. He also records his gameplay (the plot and how it is played), edits the videos to enhance viewers' enjoyment, and posts the videos on his "secret" YouTube channel. He is currently diving deep into the nuances of how YouTube algorithms affect the recommendation streams and search results, hoping to understand how to make the algorithms work better for users.

You can find Gudlavalleti on LinkedIn: Sai Gudlavalleti | LinkedIn

www.ingramcontent.com/pod-product-compliance
Lightning Source LLC
Chambersburg PA
CBHW050009230526
45465CB00003BB/1333